The burda
Cook Book No. 2

Festive Menus

200 Recipes
for Large and Small
Formal Dinners

Recipes: BURDA Test Kitchen
under the direction of Chef Ernst Birsner

Photography: Europa Farbstudio

Printed in West Germany by: Druckhaus Ernst Kaufmann, D 7630 Lahr/Schwarzwald

Copyright 1978: Aenne Burda Publishing Co., Offenburg, West Germany
1st Printing of American Edition

ISBN 3-920-158-24-5

Translated into English and
adapted for American consumers
by Eleonore Boer

Library of Congress Catalog
Card No. 77-89594

Foreword

Few things are more rewarding than having family and friends together at one's home and treating them to a festive meal. People have always enjoyed good food in good company, and sharing a meal is still an expression of friendship and appreciation, whether among primitive tribes or modern city dwellers.

The meal is often the climax of a gathering, and special occasions call for special foods served in special ways as part of the celebration. You, as a homemaker, will produce both the meals and the atmosphere for many an unforgettable event.

To make it easy for you to put a festive meal together, we have come up with more than 50 menus in this book which are all suitable for special occasions. Whether it's a wedding, an engagement party, a 50th birthday or any other cause for celebrating, celebrate it with these wonderful foods that will become part of the memory of the day. Make history with these tasty, elegant and somehow "different" dishes. If there is no special occasion, create one! How about a festive dinner for two – in a far-away place at that (because that's where some of these recipes will take you). The possibilities are unlimited because you can, of course, interchange the recipes from the different menus and create new ones – all with this one cook book that also brings you a taste of foreign lands.

Contents
Page

A Feast is also for the Eyes

Good food is to enjoy, not just for the palate but also for the eye – that's why an attractive table setting is so important. "Attractive," though, must not mean "expensive." One of the fun parts of giving a party is that you can create your own style. So what if you don't possess heirloom silver candelabras or precious China that come down to you from your grandmother! Simple dishes, used with imagination, will bespeak your good taste and delight your guests. Play with color combinations in which tablecloth, napkins and flowers are key elements. Pay attention to table settings, the correct placement of plates, glasses, serving dishes and platters. Add special interest with a candlestick or a vase. The full-color pictures on Pages 125, 129, 132 and 133 will give you some ideas on what you can do.

Whatever you do, though, remember that you want your guests to be comfortable. Don't crowd them, don't keep them from seeing each other by placing huge bouquets on the table, and don't place candlesticks and center pieces where they might be knocked over. At a formal sit-down dinner, place cards will always be appreciated; besides adding a special note, they'll also relieve you from ushering.

What to Serve When

Before your guests sit down to dinner, serve them an apéritif; this may be a Sherry, port wine, Madeira or vermouth to name a few. The apéritif is the prelude to a festive dinner. For the dinner itself, here ist a basic sequence of courses:

Course 1:	Cold appetizer
	Soup
	OR
	Soup
	Warm appetizer
Course 2:	Fish
Course 3:	Meat (Beef, pork, veal, poultry or venison)
Course 4:	Dessert (warm desserts are always being served before cold ones) Ice cream, cheeses or fruits are suitable for dessert, among others.

You can, of course, make the menu simpler by serving only the fish or the meat course, skipping one course completely. Mocha, served in demitasse cups, is always a good finale to a festive dinner.

The Right Beverages are Important!

Good food becomes even better with good drinks; the right drinks turn a meal into a feast. Depending on whether the food is refined or robust, the drink may be a sparkling wine or a hearty beer on tap, or whatever else is called for. Drinks, chosen with care, will enhance the food. The chart below will help you make the right choices. One basic rule is: Serve white wine with white meat (veal, poultry) and with fish; serve red wine with dark meat (beef, lamb, venison).

Here are some suggestions for beverages to serve with various courses:

Appetizers:
with a pâté — serve sherry, port wine or Madeira

with caviar and crustaceans — serve dry champagne or a medium dry white wine

Soups:
with creamed soups — serve a white wine

with clear bouillon or exotic soups — serve a Madeira or port wine

Fish:
with fresh-water fish such as trout, perch or whitefish — serve a dry white wine (a white Burgundy to name one), or a sparkling Moselle

with salt-water fish — serve a dry white or a rosé wine (with salmon, you may also serve a Beaujolais, which is red)

Meat:
with dark meat — serve a light, red wine such as Bordeaux, Claret or Bardolino

with white meat — serve a light, white wine; a Riesling will do fine but rosés or sparkling wines are also suitable

with venison or game birds — serve a full-bodied red wine such as Chambertin, Rioja or Burgundy

Dessert:
with warm desserts — serve a Tokaj or Sauterne (white Bordeaux)

serve a sparkling wine or sweet table wine

with cheese — serve any wine of your choice (preferably red), or a light beer

8

If the meal is concluded with a mocha, serve a celebrated brandy or a cordial with it.

A general rule for wines in a festive menu is that they should increase in quality from one course to the next.

Serving Temperatures for Wine and Champagne

White Wines	12–14° C (53–57° F) which is cellar temperature
	This goes for: Silvaner Riesling Traminer Rulaender to name a few.
Champagnes	5–7° C (41–45° F)
Red Wines	approx. 18° C (64° F) which is room temperature

The following wines should, ideally, be served at the given temperatures:

Beaujolais	12–14° C (53–57° F)
French Burgundy	16–18° C (61–64° F)
Bordeaux	18–20° C (64–68° F)

It is a good idea to have a wine thermometer at hand to ensure the correct serving temperatures.

Calories at a Glance

Breads and Fats   Calories:

Toast, white – 1 slice (30 g or 1 oz) 84

Farmer style wheat-and-rye bread – 1 slice
(45 g or 1.5 oz) 113

Butter – 1 teaspoon (5 g or 0.2 oz) 40

Margarine – 1 teaspoon (5 g or 0.2 oz) 38

Oil – 1 tablespoon (15 g or 0.5 oz) 92

Mayonnaise – 1 tablespoon
(15 g or 0.5 oz) 100

Salad Dressing, plain – 1 tablespoon
(15 g or 0.5 oz) 65

Cheese and Eggs

Camembert (45%) – 1 triangle (30 g or 1 oz) 90

Cottage cheese, creamed (125 g or 4.5 oz) 130

Cream Cheese (60 g or 2 oz) 110

Gouda Cheese (45%) – 1 serving (30 g or 2 oz) 120

Swiss Cheese (45%) – 1 serving (30 g or 1 oz) 105

Egg, 1 large – boiled 84

Egg white – 1 16

Egg yolk – 1 68

Meats and Sausages

Beef, corned – 30 g or 1 oz 50

Beef, roast – 2 thin slices (50 g or 1.8 oz) 65

Chicken, fried – 100 g or 3.5 oz 206

Chicken, stewed – 100 g or 3.5 oz 107

Ham, cooked – 1 thin slice 120

Liverwurst (calf), lean – (50 g or 1.8 oz) 135

Mortadella (pork-veal sausage) – 50 g or 1.8 oz 180

Pork, roast – 1 slice 79

Veal, roast – 1 slice 51

Seafoods

Anchovy, canned – 2 fillets   7

Caviar, red – 30 g or 1 oz 32

Caviar, genuine (black) – 30 g or 1 oz 90

Clams – 50 g or 1.8 oz 35

Cod – 30 g or 1 oz 32
Eel, smoked – 50 g or 1.8 oz 120
Fish, steamed – 100 g or 3.5 oz 90
Salmon (true), smoked – 30 g or 1 oz 54
Sardines, Norway – 1 can (125 g or 4.5 oz) 296
Shrimps – 50 g or 1.8 oz 42
Tuna, canned (in oil) – 90 g or 3 oz 170

Starchy Foods
Noodles, cooked – 1 cup 111
Potatoes, sliced and cooked – 1 cup 105
Rice, cooked – 1 cup 110

Vegetables
Artichokes – 100 g or 3.5 oz 60
Asparagus, fresh – 100 g or 3.5 oz 20
Beans, green – 100 g or 3.5 oz 33
Mushrooms, canned – 100 g or 3.5 oz 25
Mushrooms, fresh – 100 g or 3.5 oz 24
Peas, fresh – 100 g or 3.5 oz 93

Fruits and Frozen Desserts
Avocado – 1 medium (200 g or 7 oz) 400
Banana – 1 (100 g or 3.5 oz) 90
Blackberries, fresh – 100 g or 3.5 oz 48
Fruit Sherbet – 100 g or 3.5 oz 138
Ice Milk – 100 g or 3.5 oz 128
Peach – 1 (125 g or 4.5 oz) 55
Pear – 1 (125 g or 4.5 oz) 70
Pineapple, fresh – 100 g or 3.5 oz 57
Raspberries, fresh – 100 g or 3.5 oz 40
Strawberries, fresh – 100 g or 3.5 oz 39
Watermelon – 500 g or 18 oz 120

Beverages
Brandy – 1 jigger 95
Champagne-3-oz glass 75
Liqueur (cordials) – 1/2-jigger (approx.) 80
Whiskey – 1 jigger (80 proof) 100
Wine, red – 1/4 liter or 1 cup 172
Wine, white – 1/4 liter or 1 cup 154

Note: A few of the above calorie counts may differ slightly from standard American ones since they are based on continental products.

Index of Menus

Index of Menus

MENU

Cherry Fizz
Neuenburg Cheese Fondue
Orange-Wine Jelly
(not pictured)

Sparkling White Wine
or Tea

Cherry Fizz

Per drink, combine 1 part cherry liqueur, 1 part cherry brandy and 1 ice cube in a glass. Fill up with club soda, garnish with a lemon twist and serve.

Neuenburg Cheese Fondue

In fondue pot, combine grated cheese, corn starch and wine and heat on stove, stirring constantly. Crush garlic clove and add to fondue, along with the cherry brandy; season to taste with pepper and nutmeg. Keep fondue simmering over table burner. Cut the bread into bite-size pieces and serve separately. Guests spear the bread pieces and dunk them into the sauce.

Ingredients for 4 servings:
400 g (14 oz) Gruyere cheese
200 g (7 oz) Emmental cheese (or substitute first 2 ingredients with 1 lb, 5 oz Swiss cheese)
2 level tablespoons corn starch
1 cup sparkling white wine
1 clove garlic
pepper, nutmeg
3 jiggers cherry brandy
1 loaf day-old French bread

Orange-Wine Jelly

Peel oranges, removing white fibers. Cut oranges in thin slices and remove seeds. Soak gelantine in 5 tablespoons cold water for 5 minutes. Combine 1/2 cup of the wine with the sugar and heat to just boiling. Dissolve the softened gelatine in this hot mixture; add maraschino syrup and remaining wine. Alternate layers of orange slices and cherries in a glass dish, pour the liquid over them and refrigerate till it gels. Serve with whipped cream if desired.

Ingredients for 4 servings:
5 to 6 juicy oranges
4 1/2 teaspoons unflavored gelantine
1 1/2 cups white wine
1/2 cup sugar
100 g (3 1/2 oz) maraschino cherries

15

MENU

Salade du Chef (bottom, right)
Buttered Salmon Steaks with Almonds (top)
Dessert Foam with Hazelnut Brittle (bottom, left)
(pictured on opposite Page)

Sparkling White Wine

Salade du Chef

Ingredients for 4 servings:
2 hard-boiled eggs
¹/₂ honeydew melon
2 carrots; 2 tomatoes;
1 red pepper; 1 grapefruit
75 g (2.6 oz) ham
1 can asparagus (12 oz), white or
green; lettuce leaves for lining plate
50 g (1.8 oz) Roquefort cheese
3 tablespoons oil
3 tablespoons vinegar
salt, pepper, onion powder

Cut eggs in eighths and cut the following ingredients in strips: Honeydew melon, carrots, tomatoes, pepper, grapefruit and ham. Serve on a bed of lettuce leaves along with the asparagus spears. Dressing: Mix or blend together Roquefort, oil, vinegar, salt, pepper and onion powder. Pour over salad or serve separately if desired.

Buttered Salmon Steaks with Almonds

Ingredients for 4 servings:
4 fresh salmon steaks, approx.
150–200 g each (5.3–7 oz)
salt, pepper
juice from 1 lemon
2 tablespoons oil
some flour
3 tablespoons butter
3 tablespoons slivered almonds
1 lemon
some parsley

Wash salmon steaks and dab dry. Sprinkle with salt, pepper and lemon juice and set aside for 10 minutes. Heat oil in skillet. Dredge salmon steaks in flour and fry in hot oil over medium heat approx. 4 minutes on each side. Add butter to skillet and fry salmon steaks a little longer. Remove fish from skillet and keep warm. Add almond slivers to pan drippings and fry till golden brown, then sprinkle over fish on serving platter. Decorate fish with lemon slices and parsley. Serve with small potatoes, boiled with or without skins, and sprinkled with chopped dill.

Dessert Foam with Hazelnut Brittle

Ingredients for 4 servings:
1 tablespoon butter
1 tablespoon sugar
¹/₄ cup chopped hazelnuts
1 pkg (³/₄ oz) instant vanilla pudding, 1¹/₂ cups milk
¹/₂ cup whipping cream
¹/₂ jigger brandy

Melt butter and sugar in saucepan, add hazelnuts and stir till all ingredients melt together and are light brown. Turn out on oiled plate to cool, then chop the brittle coarsely. Prepare instant pudding according to package directions, using only 1¹/₂ cups milk. Stir in brandy. Whip cream and fold into pudding. Spoon into parfait serving glasses, alternating with the nut brittle; chill and serve.

MENU

Creamed Vegetable Soup, Cold
Jellied Eel
Veal in Tuna Sauce
Danish Red Pudding
with Liquid Cream
(not pictured)

Sparkling White Wine

Creamed Vegetable Soup, Cold

Ingredients for 4 servings:
4 large leeks
2 onions
$^1/_2$ cup butter
4 medium potatoes
4 cups strong chicken broth
3 cups heavy cream
salt, pepper
chives

Wash and prepare leeks, using only the white parts. Peel onions. Cut both into fine strips. Melt butter in a deep sauce-pan and sauté leek and onion strips in it lightly so they won't change color. Peel and slice potatoes and add to the sautéed vegetables. Fill up with the chicken broth and cook for approx. 30 minutes or till potatoes are done. Force soup through a strainer or purée in blender and return to saucepan. Add 2 cups heavy cream, stir and bring to a boil. Season to taste with salt and pepper; refrigerate. Whip remaining cream till just foamy, and fold into soup. Chop chives and sprinkle over soup before serving.

Jellied Eel

Ingredients for 4 servings:
1 eel, approx. 1 kg (2$^1/_4$ lb), ready to cook
1 cup dry white wine
1 cup strong meat broth
1 onion
1 bay leaf
2 cloves
5 white peppercorns
$^1/_2$ teaspoon sage
$^1/_2$ teaspoon dill
6 tablespoons wine vinegar
4 teaspoons unflavored gelatine

Wash eel, split lengthwise along center of back and divide in 2 fillets. Remove and reserve bones. Cut each fillet in 2-inch pieces. In a 6-cup saucepan, combine wine and meat broth and bring to a boil; reduce heat. Peel and slice onion and combine with fish bones, seasonings and vinegar and add to the broth. Cook over low heat for 5 minutes, then strain. Add eel pieces to hot broth and simmer (do not boil) for approx. 10 minutes. Set aside to cool and lift eel pieces out carefully with a slotted spoon. Drain and arrange on platter. Garnish with lobster tails, asparagus tips and egg or mushroom slices. When meat broth is cool, strain again, de-fat and heat once more. Soften gelatine in 5 tablespoons cold water for 5 minutes, then dissolve in the hot broth. If broth is not clear, boil it up again, remove from heat, add a stiffly beaten egg white, then bring to a boil once more. Remove from heat, let cool and filter through cheese cloth. Heat the clear broth, season to taste with salt and pour over eel pieces; refrigerate till firm.

Veal in Tuna Sauce

Peel onion and chop finely. Peel lemons, remove seeds, and cube. Peel and cube garlic clove. Heat the 6 tablespoons oil in a 3-quart saucepan, add meat and quickly sear it on all sides for 1 minute till pores close and red color disappears. Remove meat from saucepan immediately. Sauté onions in same saucepan till transparent, then add the following ingredients: Lemons, garlic, tuna, anchovies with their oil, thyme, bay leaf, pepper, white wine and broth; stir. Add meat, cover and cook over low heat for 1 1/2 hours. Remove meat and cut in slices. Tuna Sauce: Remove bay leaf from broth. Pour broth into blender and purée all solids. Beat egg yolks with salt and add 1/2 cup oil by the drop. Add tuna sauce to this mixture by the tablespoon. Season to taste with lemons and pour sauce over meat slices. Sprinkle with capers and serve.

Ingredients for 4 servings:
1 kg (2 1/4 lb) veal rump roast (without gristle)
3 large onions
3 lemons
2 cloves garlic
6 tablespoons olive oil
2 cans (7 oz ea) tuna in oil
1 can (2 oz) anchovy fillets
1/2 teaspoon thyme
1 bay leaf
some pepper
1 1/2 cups dry white wine
2 cups meat broth
2 egg yolks
some salt
1/2 cup olive oil
juice from 1/2 lemon
capers

Danish Red Pudding with Liquid Cream

Wash berries and boil in 1 1/2 cups water for 3 minutes. Strain and add enough water to make 3 cups liquid. Add sugar and bring to a boil. Dissolve corn starch in some cold water and stir into the hot liquid. Bring to a boil just once and pour immediately into serving dishes that have been rinsed with cold water; refrigerate. Serve with liquid heavy cream.

Ingredients for 4 servings:
250 g (1/2 lb, plus) raspberries or blackberries
250 g (1/2 lb, plus) red currants
1 1/2 cups water
3/4 cup sugar
1 cup heavy cream

MENU

Elegant Cream of Shrimp Soup
Savory Hawaiian Steaks
Cottage Cheese Dessert with Grapes (Insert)
(pictured on Page 21)

Beer

Elegant Cream of Shrimp Soup

Ingredients for 4 servings:
2 1/2 cans cream of shrimp soup (a 10 3/4 oz)
2 tablespoons good brandy or dry sherry
2 tablespoons heavy cream
some chopped dill

Heat soup according to label instructions; do not boil. Stir in brandy or dry sherry, sprinkle with chopped dill and serve.

Savory Hawaiian Steaks

Ingredients for 4 servings:
4 veal steaks, 100 g (approx. 3.5 oz) ea
salt, pepper, flour
2 tablespoons oil
2 tomatoes
4 slices American cheese
4 pineapple rings
1 teaspoon paprika
2 teaspoons sweet pickled honeydew melon or chopped, candied orange rind

Sprinkle steaks with salt and pepper, dredge in flour and fry in hot oil 3 minutes on each side. Cut tomatoes in half, sprinkle with pepper, dredge in flour and fry along with the steaks. Top each fried steak first with a slice of cheese, then with a pineapple ring. Return to skillet, cover and heat till cheese is melted. Dust with paprika and sprinkle with chopped, pickled honeydew melon or chopped, candied orange rind. Serve on a bed of fried rice and serve curry sauce separately in sauceboat. Recipe for curry sauce on Page 140 of Appendix.

Cottage Cheese Dessert with Grapes

Ingredients for 4 servings:
250 g (8.8 oz) creamed cottage cheese
1/2 cup milk
juice from 1/2 lemon
2 tablespoons sugar
1 jigger maraschino
250 g (8.8 oz) grapes, blue and green

Cream together cottage cheese and milk. Beat together lemon juice, sugar and maraschino and combine with the cottage cheese cream. Wash and drain grapes, remove stems and cut each grape in half, removing seeds, then mix grape halves into cottage cheese cream. Chill and serve.

MENU

Melons with Port Wine
Green Noodle Casserole
Coffee Grand Marnier
(not pictured)

Chianti

Melons with Port Wine

Ingredients for 8 servings:
4 melons (honeydew)
Port wine or sherry
some sugar

Refrigerate melons for at least 2 hours till very cold. Cut each melon in half, remove seeds and serve with a dash of port wine or sherry in it. Add sugar, if desired.

Green Noodle Casserole

Ingredients for 8 servings:
3 liters (3 quarts) salted water
500 g (1 lb, plus) green noodles
100 g (3.5 oz) Virginia style ham or Prosciutto
3 onions
2 cloves garlic
2 carrots
1 fennel bulb
4 tablespoons butter
125 g (4.4 oz) chicken or turkey livers
375 g (13 oz) ground meat loaf mix
1/2 teaspoon oregano
salt
black pepper
2 tablespoons tomato paste
1/2 cup dry white wine
1 cup meat broth
5 tablespoons butter
1 1/4 tablespoon flour
1 cup milk
1 cup heavy cream
salt, pepper, nutmeg
2 cups grated parmesan cheese
4 tablespoons butter

Fill a deep kettle with salted water and bring to a boil. Drop the green noodles into the boiling water und cook till done. Pour noodles into a colander and rinse with cold water; drain and place on a kitchen towel to absorb remaining moisture. Cube ham, peel onions and garlic and chop finely. Prepare and wash carrots and fennel and cut in small cubes. Heat butter in a shallow skillet, add the cubed ham, onions, garlic, carrots and fennel and sauté for 5 minutes. Cube livers, combine with the ground meat mix and the seasonings, add to skillet. Sauté briefly for 3 minutes, turning meat mixture over with fork several times. Add tomato paste, white wine and meat broth and cook briefly. For white sauce, heat butter in a shallow skillet, add flour and sauté till light yellow. Gradually, add milk and cream, stirring constantly. Add seasonings and cook over medium heat for 5 more minutes. In a casserole, alternate layers of meat mixture, white sauce and the green noodles. Top layer must be white sauce. Sprinkle with parmesan cheese and dot with butter. Bake in 175°C (350°F) oven for approx. 35 minutes. Serve with tossed green salad.

22

Coffee Grand Marnier

Prepare a strong coffee from first 2 ingredients and fill 8 demitasse cups ¾ full. Flame each serving with flaming Grand Marnier* as follows: Use a small (1 jigger) scoop for flaming. Pour 1 scoopful of Grand Marnier per each cup mocha. Hold scoop over flame to warm contents slightly, then ignite it and pour the flaming Grand Marnier into the demitasse cup. Repeat for remaining servings.

* If flaming Grand Marnier is not available, just pour jigger Grand Marnier into each demitasse.

Ingredients for 8 servings:
10 tablespoons ground coffee
2 cups water
16 sugar cubes
8 jiggers Grand Marnier

MENU
Shrimp Salad
Roast Duckling with Steamed Red Cabbage
and Mashed Potatoes
Cheese Platter
(not pictured)
___
Sparkling White Wine or
Full-Bodied Red Wine

Shrimp Salad

Cut pickles and green pepper in strips and combine with the drained shrimps. Marinate with pepper and lemon juice. Fold in the mayonnaise and refrigerate to develop flavor, then serve.

Ingredients for 4 servings:
1 can (4½ oz) shrimps
2 sour pickles
1 green pepper
5 tablespoons mayonnaise
pepper
lemon juice

Roast Duckling

Quarter duckling, season and quickly brown in hot oil on all sides, along with the cubed vegetables. Add tomato paste, bouillon cubes and water, cover and cook approx. 50 minutes. Core apples. Dot not peel but score on outside several times. Stuff apples with raisins and cook along with the duck portions. Thicken sauce with corn starch dissolved in some water. Serve duckling with sauce and mashed potatoes.

Ingredients for 4 servings:
1 duckling
salt, pepper
2 tablespoons oil
2 onions
2 carrots
3 tablespoons tamato paste
2 bouillon cubes
2 apples
2 teaspoons raisins
1 teaspoon corn starch

23

Steamed Red Cabbage

Ingredients for 4 servings:
2 jars (16 oz ea) red cabbage, or see basic recipe on Page 59
1 onion
2 tablespoons oil
1 cup red wine
salt
2 tablespoons fruit jam

Briefly sauté sliced onion in oil, add the red cabbage and the wine. Add seasonings and a little water and steam for approx. 30 minutes. Stir in the fruit jam and add a little vinegar to taste.

Cheese Platter

Arrange an assortment of cheeses on a platter or wooden board and garnish with blue grapes, radishes, caraway seeds and butter curls.

MENU

Manhattan Cocktail (bottom, right)
Stuffed Christmas Turkey (top)
Prince Pueckler Ice Cream Bombe
(bottom, left)
(pictured on opposite Page)

Distinguished, Elegant
White Wine
Champagne

Manhattan Cocktail

Combine 1 1/2 jiggers each sweet vermouth and whiskey (Canadian, if possible), dash Angostura bitters and 2 to 3 ice cubes. Shake and strain into cocktail glass. Impale 1 or 2 maraschino cherries on a cocktail skewer and serve along with the drink.

Stuffed Christmas Turkey

Ingredients for 8 servings:
1 Tom turkey, approx. 3 kg
(6 1/2 lb)
1 lemon
salt
2 tablespoons butter or margarine
1 teaspoon paprika
250 g (1/2 lb, plus) pork sausage
5 slices white sandwich bread
3 eggs
1/2 teaspoon onion powder
1/2 teaspoon sage
some pepper
1/4 teaspoon monosodium glutamate
1 tablespoon chopped parsley
1 tablespoon tomato paste
1 teaspoon corn starch

Sprinkle the ready-to-cook turkey with lemon juice and season with salt inside and out. Cut the bread in large cubes and mix with the beaten eggs, the pork sausage, onion powder, sage, pepper, monosodium glutamate, salt and chopped parsley. Work these ingredients into a uniform paste and stuff the neck cavity of the turkey with it. Sew cavity up. If any of the mixture is left over, stuff it into the large cavity. Melt the butter or margarine, mix with paprika, and brush the turkey with this mixture on all sides. Cover turkey with foil and roast in oven at 175°C (350°F) for 3 hours. During the last half hour, remove the foil to let turkey brown evenly. When done, transfer turkey to serving platter. Stir tomato paste into pan drippings, dissolve corn starch in a little cold water, bind pan drippings with it, then strain. Serve the strained sauce separately in a sauce boat. Arrange various vegetables around turkey on platter.

Prince Pueckler Ice Cream Bombe

Ingredients for 8 servings:
1 liter (approx. 1 qt.)
whipping cream
4 pineapple rings
2 1/2 tablespoons sugar
150 g (5.3 oz) sweet baking
chocolate
1/2 cup strawberry preserves
1 tablespoon pistachio nuts
3/4 cup powdered sugar

Chill cream. Chop pineapple rings finely, combine with sugar and cook for 5 minutes, then refrigerate. Melt baking chocolate in top of double boiler. Peel pistachio nuts and chop coarsely. Whip the refrigerated cream till bubbly, add powdered sugar and continue to whip till firm. Distribute whipped cream evenly over 3 bowls. Into one of the whipped cream portions, blend the cooled but still liquid chocolate; into another, the combined chopped pineapple rings and the pistachio nuts and into the third, the mashed strawberry preserves. Coat the inside of a thoroughly chilled mold first with the chocolate cream, following with the strawberry cream, and filling center with the pineapple cream. Close mold with aluminum foil and freeze for at least 4 hours. To unmold, run a sharp, pointed knife around edges, then dip mold in hot water for a moment and invert on serving platter. Decorate with dots of whipped cream and with maraschino cherries.

Sauerkraut-Fruit Salad (bottom, left)
Sauerbraten with Dumplings (top)
Vanilla Fluff with Blackberries
(bottom, right)
(pictured Page 28)

—

Full-Bodied Red Wine

Sauerkraut-Fruit Salad

Rinse sauerkraut briefly, then chop. Peel and cube apple and orange and mix with the chopped sauerkraut. Also mix in the hazelnuts and grapes. Chop onion, mix with tarragon, lemon juice and oil and pour this dressing over salad befor serving.

Ingredients for 4 servings:
250 g (8.8 oz) sauerkraut
1 apple; 1 orange; 1 tablespoon chopped hazelnuts
$^1/_2$ cup halved, pitted dark grapes;
Dressing: 1 onion
1 teaspoon tarragon
juice from $^1/_2$ lemon
3 tablespoons oil

Sauerbraten with Dumplings

Meat must be marinated 3 days before cooking. For marinade, wash and prepare vegetables and cut them in large cubes, approx. 1 inch. Combine with seasonings, vinegar and wine and boil for 1 minute; let cool. Place meat in this marinade and refrigerate for 3 days. Remove meat from marinade and pat dry; reserve marinade. Heat shortening in Dutch oven. Season meat with salt and pepper and quickly brown it on all sides in the hot shortening, then lift meat out of pot. Briefly sauté vegetables from marinade in meat drippings. Add tomato paste and flour and sauté for 3 minutes. Add marinade liquid and heat. Return meat to pot and cook in the liquid for 1 $^1/_2$ hours, or till done. Remove meat from pot, strain sauce and correct seasoning to taste. Serve with potato dumplings (Recipe on Page 140 of Appendix) and canned cranberries.

Ingredients for 4 servings:
750 g (26.5 oz) rump roast
1 carrot
$^1/_4$ celery root
1 onion
1 bay leaf
1 teaspoon peppercorns
6 juniper berries
$^1/_2$ cup vinegar
1 $^1/_2$ cups white wine
2 tablespoons shortening
salt, pepper
2 tablespoons tomato paste
1 tablespoon flour

Vanilla Fluff with Blackberries

Combine blackberries, sugar, lemon juice and fruit liqueur. Cook pudding according to package directions and stir in the egg yolk. Beat egg white till stiff and fold into the pudding. Let pudding cool somewhat, then spoon into serving dishes, alternating with the marinated blackberries. Chill and serve.

Ingredients for 4 servings:
250 g ($^1/_2$ lb, plus) blackberries
2 tablespoons sugar
juice from $^1/_2$ lemon
2 jiggers fruit liqueur
1 pkg (3 $^5/_8$ oz) Vanilla Pudding
1 egg, separated

MENU

Artichoke Bottoms "Nantua" (bottom)
Chinese Turkey Dinner (top)
Ice Cream Mocha (Insert)
(pictured on Page 28)

Distinguished, Elegant
White Wine

Artichoke Bottoms "Nantua"

Ingredients for 4 servings:
4 artichokes
4 tablespoons vinegar
salt
$^1/_2$ cup heavy cream
2 tablespoons lobster butter
(recipe on Page 140 of Appendix)
$2^1/_2$ teaspoons flour
1 can ($4^1/_2$ oz) shrimps
$^1/_4$ of the liquid from
canned shrimps
monosodium glutamate
cayenne pepper
juice from $^1/_4$ lemon
salt

Cut artichoke leaves down to 4 cm ($1^1/_2$ inches), remove stems and cut green leaf parts off with a sharp knife till bottoms become visible, remove the fuzzy choke with a sharp spoon. Drop artichoke bottoms immediately in 2 cups water to which vinegar and salt have been added and boil for 20 to 25 minutes. Bring cream to a boil and knead together the lobster butter and flour. Combine cream with $^1/_4$ of the shrimp liquid from can. Gradually, stir lobster butter mixture into cream and bring to a boil again. Season to taste with monosodium glutamate, cayenne pepper, lemon juice and salt. Mix in the shrimps and spoon this mixture over the hot artichoke bottoms.

Chinese Turkey Dinner

Ingredients for 4 servings:
375 g (13 oz) boned turkey breast
2 to 4 tablespoons soy sauce
1 teaspoon ground ginger
2 carrots; 1 leek; 1 zuccini
1 small fennel bulb
2 tablespoons dried, black Chinese mushrooms
4 tablespoons Chinese noodles
(bean threads)
1 cup bean sprouts
1 onion; 1 clove garlic
6 tablespoons oil
$1^1/_4$ tablespoons corn starch
salt, pepper
$^1/_4$ cup wine vinegar
2 to 3 tablespoons apricot preserves

Cut meat into thin slivers approx. $^1/_4$ inch (this is easier when meat is partially frozen). Sprinkle turkey slivers with 2 tablespoons soy sauce and some ginger and marinate at least 1 hour. Peel and prepare carrots, leeks, zuccini and fennel bulb and cut all vegetables in thin slices. Boil mushrooms in water for 1 minute; boil the bean threads for 2 minutes. Drain mushrooms and bean threads. Wash bean sprouts. Chop onion and garlic finely. Heat oil in a skillet. Combine meat and corn starch and sauté till golden brown; remove from skillet. Sauté onion and garlic in oil till yellow. Add carrots, leek, zuccini and fennel and sauté 4 minutes more. Add bean sprouts, sauté 1 minute more. Add noodles (bean threads) and mushrooms; season with salt, pepper and vinegar and mix in the apricot preserves. If desired, add $^1/_2$ cup chicken broth and 1 to 2 tablespoons soy sauce. Thicken with corn starch that has been dissolved in some cold water. Add the meat; do not cook any more, just heat. Serve with rice.

Ice Cream Mocha

Heat water but do not boil. To make mocha, dissolve powdered coffee and 1 1/2 tablespoons sugar in the hot water. Add 1/2 cup ice cubes. Whip Cream. Combine the ice cold mocha with vanilla, mocha liqueur and 1 tablespoon sugar and distribute over 4 serving glasses or coffee cups. Top each serving with a scoop of ice cream and give it a dollop of whipped cream. Garnish with chocolate sticks or chocolate covered wafers.

Ingredients for 4 servings:
7 teaspoons instant coffee powder
2 1/2 tablespoons sugar
1 teaspoon vanilla
1/2 cup heavy cream
3 jiggers mocha liqueur
4 scoops vanilla ice cream
chocolate sticks or chocolate covered wafers

MENU

Chinese Meat Fondue (top)
Strawberries "Mandorla" (bottom)
(pictured on Page 32)

Celebrated White or
Rosé Wine

Chinese Meat Fondue

Ask the butcher to cut the veal in very thin slices (or freeze partially and then cut in thin slivers). Over table burner, prepare a strong meat broth as follows: Peel onions and garlic and chop finely. Sauté in some butter till light yellow. Add the wine and boil all these ingredients till liquid has almost evaporated. Add peppercorns, about 4 cups water, monosodium glutamate and 1 cube of beef or chicken broth. Boil this mixture for approx. 10 minutes, then strain into fondue pot and season to taste, adding a dash of sherry. Serve the raw meat slivers neatly on a platter from which each guest can help himself. Individual slices are speared with fondue forks and held in the hot broth till done.

Ingredients for 4 servings:
800 g (1 lb, 12 oz) veal or pork loin
2 onions
1 clove garlic
butter
1/2 cup white wine
1 teaspoon peppercorns
1/4 teaspoon monosodium glutamate
1 cube meat broth (beef or chicken)
some sherry

Burda transfer patterns and stitch charts

burda

ABPLÄTTMUSTER 745/003

Abplättmuster Motive für eine Bluse
Motiv für Vorderteil ca. 27 x 32 cm
Motive für die Ärmel je 19 x 32 cm

745 Transfer Motifs for a blouse
Motif for front approx. 27 x 32 cm (10" x 12" ins)
Motifs for sleeves each 19 x 32 cm (7" x 12" ins)

745 Modèle à décalquer Motifs pour corsage
Motif du devant env. 27 x 32 cm.
Motif pour les manches: 19 x 32 cm chaque

authentic folklore

burda

ABPLÄTTMUSTER 666/003

Abplättmuster Stiefmütterchenmotive
1 Packung enthält 10 Motive (18 x 21 cm)

666 Transfer Pansy motifs
1 envelope contains 10 motifs (18 x 21 cm)

666 Modèle à décalquer Motifs de pensées
1 pochette contient 10 motifs (18 x 21 cm)

home decorations

burda

ZÄHLMUSTER 611/012

Zählmuster Wandbehang „Gotik"
Stichzahl 299 194, Ausführung mit Sudanwolle 140 x 90 cm, mit Kelimwolle 75 x 48,5 cm

611 Stitch chart Wall panel "Gothic"
Stitch count 299 194 Worked with Sudan wool 140 x 90 cm
Worked with Kelim wool 75 x 48,5 cm

611 Grille à points comptés Panneau mural «Art gothique»
Nombre de points 299 194. Exécution en laine Soudan 140 x 90 cm
Exécution en laine Kelim 75 x 48,5 cm

classical tapestries

To order catalogue
see reverse side.

**Burda Patterns, Inc.
Box 1568
Smyrna (Atlanta)
Ga. 30080**

Homemade Sauces for Your Fondue

1. Chop about 10 small cocktail onions finely and mix with 3 tablespoons mayonnaise, 1 or 2 tablespoons curry, 1 tablespoon apricot preserves, rum and salt.
2. Mix 2 tablespoons prepared mustard with ²/₃ cup sour cream and 2 tablespoons chopped dill. Season with salt, pepper and some gin.
3. Sprinkle a peeled garlic clove with salt, then crush it. Mix with 2 teaspoons pickled, mashed pimentos and 3 tablespoons mayonnaise. Season to taste with cayenne pepper or tabasco, making it slightly hot.

Most condiments you can buy at your supermarket. Look for tomato ketchup, chutney, sweet pickled melon, mixed pickles, cocktail onions, olives and prepared horseradish which you can mix with some whipped (not sugared) cream, or with mayonnaise. Also, have ready a lot of crisp, green salads, radishes, green peppers and tomatoes. Serve fresh French bread or potato chips along with the fondue.

The best part of this fondue is the meat broth which is seasoned to taste and served in small cups after the meal. If desired, add some Chinese noddles (bean threads) to the broth and cook till transparent; this version is popular in East Asia.

Strawberries "Mandorla"

Ingredients for 4 servings:
500 g (1 lb, plus) strawberries
4 tablespoons blanched almonds
2 tablespoons sugar
1 cup milk
1 teaspoon unflavored gelatine
¹/₂ cup heavy cream
1 jigger Kirschwasser (cherry brandy) or brandy
1 tablespoon pistachio nuts, peeled and cut

Wash strawberries, remove stems, drain and refrigerate. In a blender, cream together almonds, ³/₄ cup of the milk, and the sugar; this will take approx. 3 minutes. Sprinkle gelatine over remaining ¹/₄ cup milk and soak for 5 minutes, then stir over low heat till dissolved. Quickly stir the almond-milk mixture into the dissolved gelatine and immediately fold in the whipped cream. Season to taste with brandy or cherry brandy. Spoon the cream into serving dishes and refrigerate till it sets. Decorate with strawberries and pistachio nuts. Serve remaining strawberries separately.

MENU

Stuffed Eggs (top, left)
Smoked Pork Loin en Croute
with Vegetables (bottom)
Chocolate Pudding (top, right)
(pictured on Page 33)

Distinguished White or Rosé Wine

Stuffed Eggs

Hard-boil eggs, peel and cut in half lengthwise. Scoop out yolks and mix with the finely chopped anchovy fillets, prepared mustard, salt, pepper and soft margarine and fill this mixture into egg halves. Cut tomatoes in half and season with wine vinegar, tarragon, salt, pepper and a pinch of sugar. Place eggs on tomato halves and garnish with chopped chives. Serve on plate decorated with olives that have anchovy fillets wrapped around them.

Ingredients for 4 servings:
4 eggs; 2 anchovy fillets
1 teaspoon prepared mustard
salt, pepper
2 tablespoons margarine
4 tomatoes
wine vinegar; tarragon
pinch sugar; chives
black olives
anchovy fillets for
garnishing

Smoked Pork Loin en Croute

Sift flour into a bowl, add salt and work in the soft margarine till mixture is crumbly. Add egg and ice water, knead and refrigerate dough. Rub pork loin with ground, black pepper and crushed juniper berries. With rounded side down, brown loin lightly in skillet, set aside to cool. Roll dough into two rectangles and place meat, fat side up, on one of them. Brush edges of both dough sheets with water and cover the meat with the second one, sealing edges. From scraps of dough, cut decorations with pastry wheel and stick them on top crust. Cut two thimble-size holes in top crust and stick two small funnels of rolled aluminum foil into them for vents. Bake in preheated oven at 225°C (440°F) for 30 minutes. Let settle somewhat before carving. Serve with steamed, sliced vegetables such as zuccini, cucumbers and tomatoes; also corn cobs.

Ingredients for 4 servings:
1²/₃ cups flour
¹/₂ cup margarine
pinch salt
1 egg
2 tablespoons ice water
750 g (1 ¹/₂ lb, plus)
smoked pork loin, de-boned
pepper, juniper berries

Chocolate Pudding

Ingredients for 4 servings:
2 cups milk
1 pkg chocolate pudding mix
(3⅝ oz)
2½ tablespoons sugar
dash cinnamon
1 teaspoon instant coffee powder

Heat milk. Combine chocolate pudding mix, cinnamon and coffee powder with 5 tablespoons cold water. Remove milk from heat and stir in the pudding mixture. Bring to a boil and fill into serving dishes rinsed with cold water. Place a sheet of cellophane over each dish to prevent skins from forming; refrigerate. Decorate with vanilla sauce (recipe on Page 134 under Orange Fritters) and wafers.

MENU

Cassis Vermouth (top, right)
Stuffed Veal Breast "Vert Pre" (bottom)
Flambéed Pineapple Rings (top, left)
(pictured on Page 37)

Mature, Heavy White Wine or
Light Red Wine or Rosé

Cassis Vermouth

For each drink, combine 2 jiggers sisca (black currant liqueur) or Creme de Cassis and 1 jigger vermouth (dry). Pour this mixture into an apéritif glass and stir. Fill up with club soda.

Stuffed Veal Breast "Vert Pre"

Ingredients for 4 servings:
2 hard-boiled eggs
750 g (1½ lb) veal breast, de-boned, with a pocket cut in it
1 stale roll, sliced
200 g (7 oz) pork sausage
125 g (5 oz) fresh herbs (chervil, spinach, chives, etc.)
1 egg yolk
salt, pepper, nutmeg
onion; 1 carrot
½ cup white wine

For the stuffing, combine pork sausage, roll slices, finely chopped herbs, egg yolk, and the seasonings; mix well. Stuff this mixture into pocket in veal breast. Push 2 hard-boiled eggs into middle of stuffing, lining them up lengthwise with roast, then sew up pocket. On outside, rub meat lightly with salt and pepper. Place stuffed veal breast on rack in frying pan, skin side down, and roast at 200°C (390°F) for 30 minutes. Add the cubed onion and cubed carrot. Reduce heat to 180°C (375°F) and roast for 1 more hour. Remove veal breast from frying pan and let settle for 10 minutes before slicing. This will prevent the juice from draining out. Add white wine and some water to pan juices and cook till baked-on residues dissolve, then strain. Serve with fried potatoes and kohlrabi (recipe on Page 141 of Appendix).

Flambéed Pineapple Rings

Ingredients for 4 servings:
1 large, fresh pineapple or equiv-
alent amount of canned pineapple
rings
2 1/4 tablespoons sugar
1 tablespoon butter
3 jiggers black currant liqueur or
Creme de Cassis
2 jiggers flaming brandy
4 tablespoons heavy cream

Peel, cut and core the pineapple, leaving rings intact. If
canned, drain pineapple rings. Combine sugar and butter and
melt in a skillet (over table burner, if available). Add pineapple rings. Heat for 3 minutes. Add 3 jiggers black currant
liqueur or Creme de Cassis and 2 jiggers flaming brandy.
Ignite; shake till flames burn down. Add 4 tablespoons heavy
cream and boil till liquid is almost evaporated, then serve.

MENU

Mushroom Soup
Chicken Ficassee "Latapie"
(named after a famous French chef)
Trader's Punch
(not pictured)

Elegant White Wine

Mushroom Soup

Ingredients for 4 servings:
250 g (1/2 lb, plus) fresh mushrooms
(yellow boletes, where available)
1 slice prosciutto ham or Virginia
style smoked ham
1 tablespoon butter
1 onion
pepper, thyme
1 tablespoon flour
3 cups meat broth
2 tablespoons sour cream
1 egg yolk
herbs
lemon juice

Prepare and slice mushrooms. Dice ham and sauté
briefly in butter. Add chopped onion and sauté till yellow.
Add sliced mushrooms. Season with pepper and thyme and
dust with flour. Pour the hot broth over mushrooms and cook
over low heat for 25 minutes. Beat together sour cream and
egg yolk and bind broth with this mixture at end of cooking
time. Season to taste with chopped herbs and lemon juice.

38

Chicken Fricassee "Latapie"

Wash chicken and pat dry. Peel and slice vegetables. Melt butter in Dutch oven and add the sliced vegetables, bay leaf and thyme and sauté for 1 minute. Rub chicken with lemon juice, season with salt and pepper and place chicken and gizzards in Dutch oven. Add wine, cover and cook over low heat for 1 hour. Cut pepper pods in strips, remove pulp and boil in 3 tablespoons water for 5 minutes. Beat together cream, egg yolk and corn starch. Skin and bone chicken, strain broth and thicken with cream and egg yolk mixture. Do not cook any more. Add the cut up pepper pods and the green pepper corns, season to taste and pour sauce over chicken. Serve on platter, garnished with the goose liver pâté, grapes and mandarin orange sections.

Ingredients for 4 servings:
1 roasting chicken approx. 1 1/2 kg (3 3/4 lb), ready to cook
1 onion; 1 carrot
1/4 celery root
1/2 bay leaf
1/2 teaspoon thyme
butter
juice from 1/2 lemon
salt, pepper
1 cup white wine
1 red and one green pepper pod
1/2 cup heavy cream
1 egg yolk
1 teaspoon corn starch
1 teaspoon green peppercorns
2 slices canned goose liver pâté
a few grapes and mandarin orange sections

Trader's Punch

Dip peaches briefly in hot water and peel. Peel and core pears. Cut peaches and pears into sections and distribute over 4 serving glasses; garnish with the raspberries (frozen raspberries must first be thawed according to directions). Cover with aluminum foil and chill for at least 1 hour. Mix chilled orange and lemon juice with chilled ginger ale and pour over fruit. If desired, add 1/2 teaspoon grenadine syrup to each serving. Serve with wafers.

Ingredients for 4 servings:
2 peaches
2 pears
125 g (1/4 lb) raspberries
2 cups orange juice
juice from 1 lemon
2 cups ginger ale
2 teaspoons grenadine syrup

MENU

Cold "India" Melon (top, left)
Pork Shoulder, Black Forest Style (bottom)
Farmer Style Bread, Potato Salad, Condiments
Tangerine Cream (top, right)
(pictured on opposite Page)

Beer

Cold "India" Melon

Ingredients for 8 servings:
2 honeydew melons
(approx. 1½ lb each)
4 chicken breasts
salt
1 celery root
6 tablespoons mayonnaise
curry
juice from 1 lemon
some walnut meats and maraschino
cherries

Cut tops off melons and scoop out seeds. Cut melon balls from fruit pulp. Refrigerate melon balls and half shells. Steam chicken breasts in very little salted water for 30 minutes. In the meantime, wash and peel celery root, cut in strips and add to chicken breasts. Steam for 10 minutes. Combine mayonnaise with 1 teaspoon curry and season to taste with lemon juice and salt. Combine cubed chicken breasts, celery strips, melon balls and mayonnaise and spoon this salad into the melon halves. Decorate with nuts and maraschino cherries.

Pork Shoulder, Black Forest Style

Ingredients for 8 servings:
approx. 1½ kg (3½ lb) pickled and
slightly smoked pork shoulder
approx. 3 liters (qts) water
1 onion; 6 cloves
1 teaspoon white peppercorns
1 teaspoon juniper berries
½ teaspoon thyme
1 bay leaf

Rinse pork shoulder quickly with hot water. Pour water into a large kettle and add chopped onions, cloves, peppercorns, juniper berries, thyme and bay leaf. Bring to a boil. Add meat to broth and cook over low heat for about 10 minutes. Cover and simmer for 1½ hours. When meat is done, lift it out of broth, cut it into slices and serve along with the mixed pickles, the prepared mustard, farmer style bread and potato salad. Beer goes well with this dish. Leftovers are good for cold cuts.

40

Tangerine Cream

Ingredients for 8 servings:
1 envelope unflavored gelatine
3 eggs
4 1/2 tablespoons sugar
1 cup white wine
1/2 cup freshly squeezed tangerine juice
1 1/2 cups heavy cream
3 jiggers brandy or orange liqueur

Pour off 1/4 cup of the wine, sprinkle gelatine over it and soak for 5 minutes. In the meantime, beat together egg yolks and sugar, bring to a boil the remaining wine and the tangerine juice and add this to the egg yolk mixture. Pour mixture into top of double boiler and place over boiling water. Beat with wire whisk till creamy. Stir the softened gelatine over low heat till dissolved, then stir it into the hot egg cream. Refrigerate cream till it just begins to set. Beat egg whites into a stiff meringue and carefully fold into the cooled cream mixture. Whip cream and fold into mixture. Stir in brandy or orange liqueur and spoon into serving dishes. Garnish with tangerine sections and refrigerate till set.

MENU

Turtle Soup (bottom, left)
Roast Spring Lamb (top)
Vanilla Ice Cream with Pineapple
or Chocolate Sauce (bottom, right)
(pictured on Page 44)

Elegant White Wine or
Full-Bodied Red Wine

Turtle Soup

Ingredients for 4 servings:
8 oz can turtle soup
1 tablespoon cognac, brandy or sherry

Heat turtle soup but do not boil. Add cognac or a good brandy or old sherry to it and taste. Fill turtle soup into 4 very small cups and serve immediately.

Roast Spring Lamb

Ingredients for 4 servings:
1 kg (2 1/4 lb) leg of lamb
salt, pepper
1/4 teaspoon garlic powder or garlic salt
1 tablespoon shortening

Melt shortening in frying pan, season meat and place in pan, meaty side up, and roast in preheated oven at 220°C (430°F) for 1/2 hour. Reduce heat to 180°C (375°F) and roast for 3/4 of an hour more. Turn roast and add onion and thyme. Add broth to pan juices, boil thoroughly and strain.

Decorative Side Dishes: Chicory. Bring to a boil the lemon juice, salt and water, add the washed and halved chicories and steam for 20 minutes. Drain and sauté in margarine. Heat the canned vegetables in their liquid, drain and add some margarine.

Potato Swirls

Beat together egg yolks and 1/4 cup cold milk. Prepare 4 servings of instant mashed potatoes according to package directions but reduce total liquid to 1 1/4 cup; this includes water and milk proportionately. Combine water, milk, pepper and nutmeg in a saucepan and heat just to boiling. Beat together egg yolks and 1/4 cup milk and add to liquid in saucepan. Add enough instant mashed potatoes for 4 servings, beat till fluffy and set aside, uncovered, for 10 minutes. Then fill potato mixture into a pastry tube with a star tip and squirt small rings onto a baking sheet. Stir together evaporated milk and curry and brush mixture over potato swirls. Bake in oven at 200°C (390°F) for 10 minutes till light golden brown.

1 onion
1/2 teaspoon thyme
1 cup broth (from bouillon cubes)
For decorative side dishes:
6 chicories
juice from 1/2 lemon
1/8 teaspoon monosodium glutamate
1 1/2 cups water
1 tablespoon margarine
1/2 can green beans or whole carrots with peas (30 oz can)
for potato swirls:
instant mashed potatoes
water, milk, salt, nutmeg, pepper
2 egg yolks
1 tablespoon evaporated milk
1/2 teaspoon curry

Vanilla Ice Cream with Pineapple Sauce

Combine pineapple and lemon juice, white wine and sugar and bring to a boil. Dissolve corn starch in cold water and add to the juice and wine mixture. Bring to a boil. Season sauce to taste with orange liqueur or cherry brandy and pour over ice cream which has been divided into 4 servings.

Ingredients for 4 servings:
1 pint vanilla ice cream
1 (15 oz) can pineapple rings
juice from 1 lemon
1/2 cup white wine
1 tablespoon sugar
1 to 2 teaspoons corn starch
2 jiggers orange liqueur or cherry brandy

Variation: ... with Chocolate Sauce

Combine juice and sugar in saucepan and cook for approx. 3 minutes. Add cocoa and stir, cooking for 1 more minute. Season to taste with orange liqueur or rum and, perhaps, some cinnamon. Pour over individual ice cream servings.

Ingredients for sauce:
1/2 cup fruit syrup from canned fruits
1/2 cup sugar
2 1/2 tablespoons cocoa
1 jigger rum or orange liqueur

MENU

Meat Broth with Green Egg Sponges (top, left)
Stuffed Saddle of Veal with Vegetable Platter
and Potato Croquettes (bottom)
Danablu Pears (top, right)
(pictured on Page 45)

———

Mature White Wine
(with depth and smoothness)
or Light Red Wine or Rosé

Meat Broth with Green Egg Sponges

Ingredients for 4 servings:
125 g (¹/₄ lb) spinach
2 eggs
¹/₃ cup milk
salt, nutmeg

Finely chop spinach and mix with the beaten eggs, milk, salt and mutmeg. Pour mixture into a non-stick skillet, cover and cook for 15 minutes. Turn out on a board and cut in diamond shapes. Float diamonds on broth just before serving.

Stuffed Saddle of Veal

Ingredients for 4 servings:
1 kg (2¹/₄ lb) saddle of veal
(have backbone removed)
some butter or margarine
2 bay leaves
1 teaspoon peppercorns
1 teaspoon rosemary
salt, pepper
1 onion
2 strips smoked bacon
2 slices white sandwich bread
(crusts removed)
2 eggs
4 tablespoons blanched, grated
almonds
1 tablespoon chopped parsley
¹/₂ cup sour cream
1 teaspoon corn starch

Grease heavy duty aluminum foil and sprinkle with bay leaves, peppercorns and rosemary. Rub meat with salt and pepper and place on foil. Cube onion and smoked bacon and combine with the crumbled white bread, the eggs, almonds and parsley and mix well. Spread mixture over meat and roll meat up, jelly roll fashion. Close foil over meat roll, folding it together over top of roll and sealing tightly. Close ends of foil. Place package on a baking sheet and bake in 200°C (390°F) oven 1¹/₂ hours. Remove foil, transfer meat to platter. Combine cream and corn starch and add to drippings; boil gravy up once and serve. Side dishes: Vegetable platter and potato croquettes (recipe on Page 59).

Danablu Pears

Peel, halve and core pears; if canned, drain pears. On a wooden board, crumble camembert and process cheese with fork and mix both cheeses. Stir some chopped parsley, ground caraway and a very small amount of paprika or cayenne pepper into cheese mixture. If desired, add a little sherry or brandy. Toast bread slices and arrange on a baking sheet. Place a pear half on each bread slice, cavity side up, and cover each half with some of the cheese mixture. Bake in oven at 220°C (430°F) for 10 minutes. Dust with paprika or cayenne pepper and serve on lettuce leaves.

Ingredients for 4 servings:
2 fresh pears or 4 canned pear halves
125 g (¼ lb) camembert cheese
1 triangle pasteurized process cheese
parsley
some caraway seeds, some paprika or cayenne pepper
a few drops sherry or brandy (optional)
4 slices white bread
some lettuce leaves

MENU
Oxtail Soup with Spring Vegetables (top, right)
Fried Veal Sweetbreads à la Queen (center)
Fruit Cocktail "Grand Marnier" (top, left)
(pictured on Page 49)

Celebrated White Wine

Oxtail Soup with Spring Vegetables

Wash and prepare celery root, carrot, leek (without the green leaves) and cube these vegetables. Melt butter in a soup kettle and sauté vegetables in it for 10 minutes till light golden yellow. Add sherry. Pour the clear oxtail soup over it and heat; do not cook. Serve with French bread or rolls.

Ingredients for 4 servings:
¼ celery root
1 carrot
1 leek
1 tablespoon butter
¼ cup sherry
2 cups clear oxtail soup
(recipe on Page 141 of Appendix)
(or mock-turtle-soup)

Fried Veal Sweetbreads à la Queen

Ingredients for 4 servings:
500 g (1 lb, plus) veal sweetbreads
salt, pepper
juice from 1/2 lemon
some flour
1 onion
1 tablespoon chopped
parsley
1 sour pickle
4 tablespoons butter
1 cup red wine
2 jiggers Madeira
3 teaspoons brown gravy mix
1 pkg. frozen green peas (10 oz)
4 patty shells (frozen)
1/2 teaspoon curry

Place sweetbreads in slightly salted water, bring to a boil, cover and simmer for 15 minutes. Set aside to cool. Cut sweetbreads in 1/2-inch slices and season with salt, pepper and lemon juice, then turn them in flour and fry in the hot butter for 4 minutes on each side. Transfer to a hot platter. Chop onion, parsley and pickle finely and sauté in the drippings for 2 minutes. Pour this mixture over the sweetbread slices. In a saucepan, combine red wine and Madeira and boil for 1 minute. Thicken with some brown gravy mix and pour this sauce over the sweetbread slices. Bake patty shells according to directions. Cook frozen peas according to directions and season lightly with curry. Spoon peas into patty shells.
Note: To avoid discoloration, soak sweetbreads in water for 1 to 2 hours before cooking.

Fruit Cocktail "Grand Marnier"

Ingredients for 4 servings:
4 cups fresh fruit or 1 kg (2 1/4 lb)
canned fruit cocktail
1/2 cup fruit juice
2 teaspoons vanilla
2 tablespoons sugar
1/4 teaspoon ground
ginger or cardamom
juice from 1/2 lemon
1 tablespoon sugar
2 or 3 jiggers Grand Marnier

Pick fresh fruits over, prepare, wash and drain. Depending on size, use fruits whole or cut up. Canned fruits must be drained. In a small saucepan, combine 1/2 cup fruit juice (apple or grape), sugar, lemon juice and ginger or cardamom and bring to a boil. Remove from heat, stir in vanilla, set aside to cool. Add Grand Marnier and combine this mixture with the fruits. Refrigerate 1 hour and serve with whipped cream.

MENU

Red Day Cocktail

Mix 2 parts Sangrita and 1 part gin and serve in a cocktail glass over the rocks. Offer lemon slices with this drink.

Suckling Pig

with Tossed Green Salad, Farmer Style Bread and Condiments

Ingredients for 4 servings:
Approx. 2 kg (4 1/2 lb) suckling pig
salt, pepper
1 teaspoon rosemary
2 cloves garlic
10 juniper berries
1 cup dark beer
1 teaspoon butter
2 tablespoons oil
1 onion

Wash meat and pat dry. Rub with salt and pepper. Combine beer, butter, rosemary, crushed garlic clove, juniper berries, salt and plenty of ground black pepper and simmer this mixture for 10 minutes. Brush suckling pig with this broth, especially on the inside. Place suckling pig in oil in frying pan, skin side down. Roast in preheated oven at 175°C (350°F) for 45 minutes. Brush with the marinade liquid several times during roasting. Turn meat and arrange onion cubes around it. Roast for another 40 minutes. Serve with sweet-sour pumpkins (recipe on Page 142 of Appendix), other condiments of your choice, farmer style bread and tossed green salad.

Cold Raspberry Soup

Ingredients for 4 servings:
750 g (1 1/2 lb) raspberries or black-berries
1 cup white wine
2 cups water
4 1/2 tablespoons sugar
3 tablespoons corn starch
juice from 2 lemons

In a saucepan, combine and bring to a boil the wine, water and sugar. Beat together corn starch and water and add to saucepan; boil up once more while stirring. To cool quickly, place saucepan in cold water, removing lid. In the meantime, pick berries over, wash and drain them, then purée in blender or force through strainer. Add berry purée to wine soup along with lemon juice. Cover and refrigerate till very cold.

50

MENU

Clear Broth with Egg Sponges
(bottom, left)
Stuffed Veal Chops
with New Potatoes and Kohlrabi (top)
Strawberries "Ninon" (bottom, right)
(pictured on Page 53)

Hearty, Distinguished
White Wine

Clear Broth with Egg Sponges

Beat together eggs, milk, salt and some nutmeg. Pour mixture into a non-stick skillet. Cover and allow to curdle over low heat for 20 minutes. Prepare meat broth from cubes. Turn egg mixture out on a board and cut into diamond shapes. Float these egg sponges on the broth just before serving.

Ingredients for 4 servings:
3 eggs
1/2 cup milk
salt, nutmeg
2 cups meat broth made from cubes

Stuffed Veal Chops

Combine ground veal with mustard, chopped herbs and egg yolk. Stuff veal cutlets with equal amounts of this mixture and sprinkle on outside with salt and pepper, then dredge in flour, dip in beaten egg white and, last, in bread crumbs. Heat the butter slowly in a skillet, place cutlets in the hot butter and fry till done, turning once. Serve on a preheated platter. Add the remaining chopped herbs to pan drippings and pour drippings and herbs over cutlets. Serve with French fries or new potatoes and kohlrabi or asparagus as side dishes.

Ingredients for 4 servings:
4 thick veal chops (approx. 150 g or 5 oz ea) with a pocket cut in each
125 g (1/4 lb) ground veal
1 teaspoon prepared mustard
1 tablespoon chopped herbs
1 egg
salt, pepper, flour
bread crumbs
1 tablespoon butter or margarine
1 tablespoon chopped herbs

Strawberries "Ninon"

Chill 4 serving dishes in freezer for approx. 10 minutes. Then, distribute vanilla ice cream over serving dishes. Wash and drain strawberries and arrange them around each serving of ice cream. Cut pineapple rings in half and arrange them over ice cream. Garnish each serving with a strawberry leaf or a wafer. Beat raspberry preserves with 1/2 cup pineapple syrup and pour some of this sauce around each serving, then serve immediately.

Ingredients for 4 servings:
500 g (1 lb, plus) fresh strawberries
4 pineapple rings
1 1/4 cup ice cream (vanilla)
2 tablespoons raspberry preserves

MENU

Cold Spanish Soup (Gazpacho)
Beef-Pork Kabobs
Potatoes Baked in Foil
Variety Salad
Ice Cream Cup with Fruits
(not pictured)

Cold Spanish Soup (Gazpacho)

Ingredients for 8 Servings:
2 cups tomato juice
4 cups good, strong meat broth without fat
6 tablespoons olive oil
juice from 5 lemons
approx. 20 ice cubes
3 cloves garlic; 4 onions
1 1/2 long (or 3 short) salad cucumbers
4 green peppers
2 fennel bulbs
salt, pepper

Stir together tomato juice, meat broth, olive oil, lemon juice and ice cubes and pour mixture into a tureen. Peel and grate garlic cloves. Peel onions and salad cucumbers, prepare and wash green peppers and fennel bulbs and cube all vegetables. Add cubed vegetables to liquid ingredients in tureen and chill for 1 hour, then season to taste with salt and pepper. Serve the gazpacho with toast or French bread.

Beef-Pork Kabobs

Ingredients for 8 servings:
500 g (1 lb, plus) beef loin
500 g(1 lb, plus) pork loin
250 g (1/2 lb, plus) large mushrooms
8 small tomatoes
10 strips smoked bacon
2 red peppers
2 green peppers
16 small, raw pork links

Cube meat, combine with 4 tablespoons oil and 1 tablespoon lemon juice, some black pepper, 2 crushed, unpealed garlic cloves and 2 crushed bay leaves and marinate for 1 hour, then string on skewers, alternating with the other ingredients (bacon must be cut in squares and peppers must be quartered). Brush with oil and broil or barbecue for 12 to 15 minutes on each side. After 10 minutes, brush with a commercial barbecue sauce. Note: For rare meat, string pieces close together; for crisp, well-done meat, leave small spaces.

Variety Salad

Ingredients for 8 servings:
6 tomatoes
1 bunch radishes
1 long salad cucumber or 2 short salad cucumbers
1 red pepper; oil, vinegar
2 tablespoons chopped dill
pepper
prepared mustard; salt

Clean, wash and cube the vegetables. Combine 6 tablespoons oil, 4 tabelspoons vinegar, finely chopped dill, some pepper, prepared mustard and salt and pour this dressing over remaining ingredients. Toss and let stand for a moment before serving.

54

Baked Potatoes in Foil

Brush potatoes with oil, sprinkle with salt and wrap in heavy duty aluminum foil. Bake in oven at 225°C (440°F) or on barbecue.

Ingredients for 8 servings:
8 large mealy potatoes
2 tablespoon oil; salt

Ice Cream Cup with Fruits

In a saucepan, combine pineapple and lemon juice and bring to a boil. Beat together rum and corn starch and add to hot liquid, stir and bring to a boil once more. With a spoon that has been dipped in hot water, scoop ice cream from package and distribute to individual serving dishes or champagne glasses, alternating ice cream and fruits in each serving. Pour the chilled pineapple sauce over it.

Ingredients for 8 servings:
1 pint vanilla ice cream
1 can (20 oz) pineapple rings
$^3/_4$ cup maraschino cherries, juice from 1 lemon
1 jigger rum
1 tablespoon corn starch

MENU

Clear Meat Broth
with Ham Dumplings (top, left)
Paprika Roast with Mashed
Potatoes and Kraut-Salad (bottom)
Jellied Fruits (top, right)
(pictured on Page 57)

Full-Bodied Red Wine

Clear Meat Broth with Ham Dumplings

Peel and chop onion, cube ham. Remove crusts from bread slices and pour cream over bread. Sauté onions in margarine until light yellow; add ham, cream-soaked bread, egg, flour and chopped parsley; mix well. Season to taste with some salt, nutmeg and pepper. Bring to a boil 1 quart salted water and drop dumpling dough in by the teaspoonfuls. Simmer only, do not cook. As soon as dumplings float to surface, remove them from water. Serve in clear broth.

Ingredients for 4 servings:
1 onion
3 slices cooked ham
2 slices white sandwich bread
2 tablespoons heavy cream
1 tablespoon margarine
1 egg, $^1/_2$ tablespoon flour
1 tablespoon chopped parsley;
some salt, nutmeg
white pepper
4 cups meat broth

55

Paprika Roast

Ingredients for 4 servings:
750 g (1 1/2 lb) fresh pork loin roast
2 onions
3 green peppers
1 apple
1 clove garlic
1 lemon
oil
2 cups white or red wine (or water)
paprika
salt, pepper, caraway seed

In a Dutch oven, heat 2 tablespoons oil. Rub meat with salt, pepper and caraway seeds and place in the hot fat. Brown lightly on all sides. In the meantime, peel onions and cut them into strips. Remove the browned meat from pot. Sauté onions in same fat till light brown. Remove pot from heat and add 3 1/4 tablespoons paprika. Mix all ingredients well. Add 2 cups of water or red or white wine and return pot to heat. Return meat to sauce, cover and cook over low heat for 1 1/2 hours. Quarter peppers, remove seeds and pulp and cut pepper pods in strips. Peel garlic clove and crush with some salt. Quarter the apple and cut each quarter in thin slices. Wash lemon and cut a thin peel from one quarter of it. Cut this peel into very fine strips. After first half of cooking time, add peppers, garlic, apple and lemon peel. When meat is done, cut it in slices and serve with mashed potatoes and kraut salad (recipe on Page 126).

Jellied Fruits

Ingredients for 4 servings:
4 cups mixed fruit
(canned fruit cocktail)
1 cup fruit syrup
1/2 cup white wine
juice from 1/2 lemon
1 to 2 tablespoons sugar
1 teaspoon vanilla
1 tablespoon sugar
1 envelope unflavored gelatine
2 jiggers apricot liqueur

Drain fruit and distribute over 4 serving dishes. Sprinkle gelatine over 5 tablespoons cold water and soak for 5 minutes. Bring white wine, fruit juice, lemon juice and sugar to a boil. Turn off heat and add the softened gelatine to the hot liquid and stir till dissolved, approx. 2 minutes. Add vanilla and apricot liqueur; stir. Pour fruit sauce over fruits. Chill till firm and serve with whipped cream. The whipped cream may be given special flavors by mixing it with one of the following: Vanilla, toasted almond slivers, instant chocolate drink powder, egg nog, chopped ginger or instant coffee powder with some sugar.

MENU

Shrimp Cocktail
Roast Turkey with Steamed
Red Cabbage and Potato Croquettes
Vanilla Ice Cream with
Hot Raspberry Sauce
(not pictured)

Hearty White Wine

Shrimp Cocktail

Ingredients for 8 servings:
2 cans (4 1/2 oz ea) shrimps
lettuce leaves
1 cup heavy cream
4 tablespoons tomato ketchup
juice from 1/2 lemon
1/2 teaspoon paprika or pepper
2 teaspoons brandy
salt to taste
2 teaspoons grated horseradish (optional)
2 lemons
chopped parsley

Line 8 serving dishes with lettuce leaves and arrange the drained shrimps over leaves. Whip cream; do not add sugar. Fold the following ingredients carefully into the whipped cream: Ketchup, lemon juice, pepper, brandy, salt and horse-radish. Season with salt to taste and pour cream over shrimp servings. If desired, decorate with olive and lemon slices as well as chopped parsley and mushrooms. Toast and butter may be served along with this seafood cocktail.

Roast Turkey

Ingredients for 8 servings:
1 turkey, approx. 3 kg
(6 1/2 lb, ready to cook
1 lemon
salt
2 tablespoons butter or margarine
1 teaspoon paprika
250 g (1/2 lb, plus) pork sausage
5 slices white sandwich bread
3 eggs
1/2 teaspoon onion powder
1 teaspoon sage
some pepper
1/4 teaspoon monosodium glutamate
1 tablespoon chopped parsley

Sprinkle turkey with lemon juice and season with salt inside and out. Cut the bread in large cubes and mix with beaten eggs, pork sausage, onion powder, sage, pepper, monoso-dium glutamate, salt and chopped parsley. Work all these in-gredients together and stuff into neck cavity of turkey; sew up. If any of the stuffing is left over, stuff it into the large cavi-ty. Melt butter or margarine and stir in the paprika. Brush turkey well on all sides with this mixture. Cover turkey with aluminum foil and roast in oven at 175°C (350°F) approx 3 hours. During the last hour of roasting, remove foil to allow turkey to brown nicely. Serve on platter, surrounded with baked apple halves which have been topped with cranberries. Side dishes: Steamed red cabbage and potato croquettes (re-cipes follow).

58

Steamed Red Cabbage

Peel and slice onion and apples; steam. Add the finely shredded cabbage and season with salt and pepper. Add meat broth and cook till cabbage is done. Dissolve corn starch in a little cold water and bind the liquid with it, adding raspberry juice and vinegar.

Ingredients for 8 servings:
1 tablespoon butter or margarine
1 onion
4 apples
1 head red cabbage
2 bay leaves
4 cloves
1 cup meat broth (made from cubes)
4 tablespoons raspberry or blackberry syrup
4 tablespoons vinegar
2 tablespoons corn starch

Potato Croquettes

Mash the freshly boiled potatoes with mixer, adding butter or margarine, nutmeg, egg yolks and chopped herbs; season to taste with salt. Place this mixture on a floured board and shape it into long rolls. Cut rolls into pieces of desired lengths and dip these first in egg whites, then in bread crumbs and fry in deep fat at 175°C (350°F) for approx. 3 minutes. Remove from fat and drain on paper towels.

Ingredients for 8 servings:
20 medium potatoes (mealy)
salt
2 tablespoons butter or margarine
nutmeg; 4 eggs, separated
2 tablespoons chopped herbs
flour, bread crumbs

Vanilla Ice Cream with Hot Raspberry Sauce

Scoop ice cream into a chilled dish (if you have no scoop, use a tablespoon dipped in hot water); place in refrigerator. In saucepan, combine water and sugar and boil for 1 to 2 minutes. Add frozen raspberries, cover and thaw. Beat together lemon and orange juice and the corn starch and pour this mixture over raspberries. Bring these ingredients to a boil and cook briefly. Add cherry brandy or brandy; stir. Pour this sauce into a sauce boat and serve hot with the ice cream.

Ingredients for 8 servings:
1 quart vanilla ice cream
2 cups water
4 1/2 tablespoons sugar
2 pkgs frozen raspberries (1 lb and 5 oz total)
juice from 2 lemons and 2 oranges
2 tablespoons corn starch
2 jiggers cherry brandy or brandy

59

MENU

Clear Oxtail Soup (top, left)
Alsatian Meat Pie (bottom)
Raw Vegetable Platter
Vanilla Ice Cream with Brandy Sauce (top, right)
(pictured on opposite Page)

Distinguished Red Wine

Clear Oxtail Soup

Ingredients for 4 servings:
1 can clear oxtail soup (if not available, see basic recipe on Page 141 of Appendix
some dry sherry or brandy

Heat the clear oxtail soup, add a dash of dry sherry or brandy and serve with cheese fours.

Alsatian Meat Pie

Ingredients for 4 servings:
300 g (10½ oz) pork butt
200 g (7 oz) veal cutlet
1 onion
2 tablespoons chopped chervil or parsley
1½ teaspoon pâté seasoning (see Page 3 of Appendix)
some nutmeg
pepper
5 tablespoons brandy
salt
2 pkgs refrigerated butterflake rolls
1 pkg refrigerated crescent rolls
3 eggs
½ cup sour cream

Remove gristle and cut meat in small cubes, approx. ³/₄ inch. Peel onion, wash herbs and chop both finely. Combine herbs, seasonings (except salt) and brandy and marinate the meat in this mixture overnight. Separate butterflake rolls into disks, leaving disks in pairs with butter between them. Line a greased 9 to 10 inch spring form or pie pan with these double disks, pushing them together to close gaps. Prick with fork several times. Remove meat cubes from marinade, add some salt and arrange meat in center of dough base. Brush edges of dough with water. Unroll crescent roll sheets but ignore perforations. Cover meat pie with this dough, sealing the 2 sheets together and cutting dough at corners to adjust to round pan. Cut a small hole in center of pie for a vent. Brush top of pie with beaten egg yolk and some milk. Bake in 220°C (430°F) oven for 25 minutes. Beat together 2 eggs, sour cream and pepper and pour this mixture into pie through top opening, reduce heat to 180° C (375° F) and bake for another 25 minutes. Serve meat pie with a platter of raw vegetables and your favorite dressing. Note: Instead of refrigerated rolls, frozen phillo (or fillo) dough can be used.

Vanilla Ice Cream with Brandy Sauce

Ingredients for 4 servings:
2 oranges; 1 banana
½ cup white wine
2 tablespoons sugar
2 jigger brandy
1 pint vanilla ice cream

Peel and cube oranges and banana. Combine and bring to a boil white wine and sugar. Add brandy and fruits. Distribute ice cream among 4 serving dishes and serve the warm brandy sauce along the with ice cream.

MENU

Daiquiri on the Rocks
Fondue Bourguignonne
Orange Sections with Yogurt Sauce
(pictured on back cover)
——
Heavy Red Wine
(Burgundy)

Daiquiri on the Rocks

In a tall glass, combine 3 ice cubes, juice from ¹/₂ lemon, 1 to 2 tablespoons grenadine syrup and 2 jiggers rum. Stir and fill up with club soda.

Foundue Bourguignonne

Ingredients for servings:
1 kg (2 ¹/₄ lb) beef filet mignon
1 liter (quart) oil or 1 kg (2 ¹/₄ lb) shortening

Remove membranes from filet mignon. Cut meat in 1-inch cubes, pile it on a board and serve raw as part of the fondue. Heat oil or shortening in fondue pot on stove, then place it over fondue burner to keep hot and bubbling. Meat cubes will be speared individually with fondue forks and cooked in the hot fat for 3 to 4 minutes. Serve French bread, French fries, pickles, cocktail onions, pitted black olives and other condiments as accompaniments. Also, serve a variety of sauces. Recipes for 4 fondue sauces follow:

Cold Avocado Sauce

Ingredients for 4 servings:
2 ripe avocados
6 tablespoons blanched almonds
2 tablespoons wine vinegar
some onion and garlic powder
salt, pepper

Cut avocados in half lengthwise, remove seeds. Scoop out fruit pulp with a small spoon. In a blender, combine avocado pulp and remaining ingredients and purée. Serve chilled.

62

Sauce Chateaubriand

Wash green onions and mushrooms and chop both ingredients coarsely; combine in saucepan with bay leaf, thyme and white wine. Cook till liquid is reduced to approximately $1/3$ cup, then strain. Stir in bouillon crystals and butter and do not cook any more. Serve hot.

Ingredients for 4 servings:
3 green onions
50 g (1$3/4$ oz) fresh mushrooms
$1/2$ bay leaf
$1/4$ teaspoon thyme
1 cup dry white wine
1 level teaspoon beef
bouillon crystals
$1/2$ cup sweet butter

Cumberland Sauce

Peel orange very thinly and cut the thin peel in fine strips. Combine strips with red wine and ginger and cook for 10 minutes. Set aside to cool. Squeeze the juice from $1/2$ lemon and 1 orange; combine with currant jelly, prepared mustard and horseradish. Add the cooled wine broth and season to taste with cayenne pepper. Serve chilled.

Ingredients for 4 servings:
1 orange
$1/2$ cup red wine
1 teaspoon ginger
1 cup currant jelly
$1/2$ lemon
1 teaspoon prepared
mustard
1 tablespoon grated horseradish,
fresh or prepared
some cayenne pepper

Truffle-and-Goose-Liver Mousse

Cream goose liver pâté with a wooden spoon, then combine with the finely chopped truffles and their liquid. Last, stir in the cognac.

Ingredients for 4 servings:
1 can (4$1/2$ oz) goose liver pâté
1 can (1$1/4$ oz) French truffles
1 tablespoon cognac

Orange Sections with Yogurt Sauce

With a sharp knife, remove orange peel and the underlying white fibers. Scoop fruit pulp out of connecting tissues, remove seeds, distribute orange pulp among 4 dessert dishes and sprinkle with orange liqueur. Let stand for 10 minutes. Stir together yogurt and powdered sugar and spoon this sauce over orange pulp servings. Sprinkle with lightly toasted almond slivers and serve with wafers or shortbread cookies if desired. Variation: Yogurt sauce may be sweetened with brown sugar instead of powdered sugar.

Ingredients for 4 servings:
8 oranges
2 jiggers orange liqueur
$1/2$ cup yogurt
2$1/4$ tablespoon powdered sugar
1$1/2$ tablespoons slivered almonds

MENU

Chicken Broth "Palmito" (top, right)
Roast Saddle of Lamb with Vegetables (bottom)
Snow Eggs with Vanilla Sauce (top, left)
(pictured on opposite Page)

Celebrated White Wine or
Velvety Red Wine

Chicken Broth "Palmito"

Ingredients for 4 servings:
3 cups chicken broth (canned or from cubes)
$1/2$ of a 16-oz can hearts of palm;
$1/2$ cup dry white wine; 1 tablespoon chopped chervil
some chopped chives

Prepare chicken broth from cubes according to directions. Drain hearts of palm and add to broth along with the wine and chervil. Sprinkle with chopped chives just before serving.

Roast Saddle of Lamb

Ingredients for 4 servings:
1 kg (2 1/4 lb) saddle of lamb (double loin portion)
2 cloves garlic
salt, pepper
2 tablespoons oil
1 onion
1 carrot
1 cup meat broth

Have butcher separate loin strips from back bone and remove membranes. Before cooking place loin strips back into position and firmly tie saddle of lamb together with string, securing ends with knots. Peel and grate garlic, mix with salt and pepper and rub meat with this mixture. Heat oil in a roasting pan and brown meat in it, fat side down. Arrange meat in roasting pan with backbone in center and loin strips at sides, and roast in 200° (390°F) oven for 60 minutes, adding onion and carrot after the first 15 minutes. Remove meat from pan and add the cup of meat broth to pan juices, bring to a boil and strain before serving.

Snow Eggs with Vanilla Sauce

Ingredients for 4 servings:
2 eggs, separated
pinch salt
5 tablespoons sugar,
1 1/2 cups milk
1 teaspoon vanilla
1 level tablespoon corn starch,
4 tablespoons cold milk

Beat egg whites till stiff, adding salt. Beat in sugar. Heat milk but do not boil. Add vanilla. With a tablespoon, cut egg shaped dumplings from the meringue and place them in the hot vanilla sauce. Cover and simmer (do not boil) over very low heat for 4 minutes; lift out with a slotted spoon. Beat egg yolks with 4 tablespoons cold milk and 1 tablespoon corn starch and add to the hot milk, stirring over low heat till mixture thickens. Refrigerate vanilla sauce, pour into a shallow serving dish and top with the snow eggs before serving.

MENU

Cold Roast Beef Cuts

Ingredients for 4 servings:
approx. 800 g (1 lb, 10 oz) beef
tenderloin roast
salt, pepper
4 tablespoons oil
For the sauce:
1/2 cup mayonnaise
1 sour pickle
some parsley
1 hard-boiled egg
2 anchovies
some capers, onion and paprika

Season meat with salt and pepper and quickly brown on all sides in the hot oil at 200°C (390°F); reduce heat in oven to 160°C (325°F) and roast meat for 25 minutes for rare, 40 minutes for medium rare. Let cool and slice. For remoulade: Chop pickle, parsley, hard-boiled egg, anchovies and capers; grate a piece of onion and combine these ingredients with mayonnaise and paprika; serve sauce with the cold cuts.

Artichoke Hearts "Verdurette"

Ingredients for 4 servings:
500 g (1 lb, plus) pickled artichoke
hearts
some chives and parsley
and other herbs such as chervil and
tarragon
2 hard-boiled eggs
6 tablespoons oil
3 tablespoons vinegar
salt, pepper

Chop herbs. Peel and cube eggs and combine with artichoke hearts. Stir in the oil and vinegar and season with salt and pepper to taste.

Vegetable Salad

Ingredients for 4 servings:
2 cups raw vegetables, cubed (celery
roots, carrots, turnips)
1 cup canned vegetables (peas, green
beans)
some fresh mushrooms
salt, pepper, monosodium glutamate
1/2 cup mayonnaise

Steam the raw vegetables in slightly salted water till done; drain. Combine with the drained, canned vegetables and season to taste with salt, pepper and monosodium glutamate. Gently fold in the mayonnaise; chill and serve.

66

Pagoda Salad

Cut ham and chicken in strips and combine with the halved cocktail onions and pimento strips. Make a dressing of mayonnaise, ketchup and horseradish and toss salad in it. Garnish with cherries and mandarin orange sections.

Ingredients for 4 servings:
150 g (5 oz) cooked ham
150 g (5 oz) cooked chicken or veal
10 cocktail onions
4 tablespoons pickled pimento strips
1/2 cup mayonnaise
2 tablespoons grated fresh (or prepared) horseradish
2 tablespoons tomato ketchup; some tart cherries (fresh or canned)
some mandarin orange sections for garnishing

Olive-Mushroom Salad

Cut olives in half and combine with the sliced, drained mushrooms. Season with lemon juice, grated garlic, cubed onion and chopped parsley and sprinkle with a little salt. Toss and serve chilled.

Ingredients for 4 servings:
approximately 20 stuffed green olives
1 can (4 oz) mushrooms
1/2 lemon; 1/2 clove garlic
1 small onion or 2 green onions
some parsley and salt

Spring Salad

Cut bologna in strips, slice tomatoes and pickles. Combine these ingredients and pour enough of the sour pickle marinade over them to suit your taste. Stir in the prepared mustard, chopped onion and chopped garlic. Season to taste with pepper and salt and stir in some oil. Sprinkle with chopped chives and capers and serve.

Ingredients for 4 servings:
250 g (1/2 lb, plus) bologna
500 g (1 lb, plus) tomatoes
2 sour pickles
1 teaspoon prepared mustard
1 small onion
1 clove garlic
pepper, salt
3 tablespoons oil
some chopped chives
1 tablespoon capers

Salad "Niçoise"

Peel and cube potatoes. Drain green beans. Peel the first 5 tomatoes, remove seeds and cube. Peel and cube onion, chop anchovies coarsely. Combine all these ingredients plus the olives and capers and grate the garlic over them. Add olive oil and vinegar and season to taste with salt and pepper. Toss and sprinkle with chopped parsley and tarragon. Cut the tops off the last 8 tomatoes, scoop out the pulp and stuff tomatoes with the vegetable salad. Top each tomato with a slice of hard-boiled egg.

Ingredients for 4 servings:
4 medium potatoes, boiled in their jackets
500 g (1 lb, plus) canned green beans; 5 tomatoes
10 stuffed green olives
1 tablespoon capers
6 to 8 anchovies
1 small onion
1 clove garlic
6 tablespoons olive oil
4 tablespoons vinegar
salt, pepper, tarragon
8 tomatoes
2 eggs, hard-boiled

Ice Cream Torte

Ingredients for 4 servings:
4 egg whites
1/4 lemon
dash salt
4 tablespoons sugar
2 cups heavy cream
2 teaspoons vanilla
2 tablespoons sugar
2 jiggers cherry brandy or rum
2 1/2 tablespoons cocoa

Separate eggs and beat egg whites with lemon juice and salt till meringue stands up in soft peaks; last, beat in 4 tablespoons sugar. Whip cream, adding 2 tablespoons sugar and 2 teaspoons vanilla. Fold in the beaten egg whites. Divide mixture in 2 equal portions and mix cherry brandy or rum into one, cocoa into the other. Line a 9 1/2-inch (24 cm) spring form with wax paper and spoon both cream portions into it, spreading one on top of the other. Freeze for several hours. Remove from spring form and serve on platter; garnish in any way desired.

MENU
Vegetable Dip "Niçoise" (bottom, right)
Roast Pork (top)
with Risi-Bisi (Rice and Green Peas)
Hazelnut Cream (bottom, left)
(pictured on opposite page)

Hearty White Wine

Vegetable Dip "Niçoise"

Ingredients for 6 servings:
1 bunch celery
2 carrots
1/4 head cauliflower
2 tomatoes
1 green pepper
4 tablespoons margarine
4 tablespoons corn oil
2 cloves garlic
1 onion
1 can (2 oz) anchovy fillets

Prepare and wash vegetables, cut in strips and arrange attractively on a large platter. Heat the margarine over a table burner and sauté the finely chopped garlic and onion in it for approx. 2 minutes. Add the coarsely chopped anchovies and stir. Keep this sauce warm over table burner. Have guests spear raw vegetables with fondue forks and dip them in the hot sauce.

Roast Pork with Risi-Bisi*
* Rice and Green Peas

Ingredients for 6 servings:
750 g (1 1/2 lb, plus) pork roast
1 onion
1 carrot
1 leek
1/4 celery root, some salt
1/4 teaspoon crushed thyme
some pepper and paprika
1/2 cup red wine
oil for frying

Prepare and wash onion, carrot, leek and celery and chop coarsely. Pour some oil into a frying pan and add the cubed vegetables. Sprinkle meat with salt, thyme, pepper and paprika and roast on lower rack of oven at 220°C (430°F) for 1 1/2 hours. Cover with aluminium foil after the first 10 minutes. Add 1/2 cup red wine or water after 45 minutes from start of roasting time. When meat is done, strain sauce, cut roast in slices and serve with cooked rice into which green pears are mixed.

68

Hazelnut Cream

Ingredients for 6 servings:
1/2 cup grated hazelnuts
1 teaspoon instant coffee powder or
2 to 3 teaspoons instant chocolate
 powder; 250 g (1/2 lb) ricotta cheese
4 tablespoons sugar
1 cup heavy cream
1 jigger cherry brandy, rum or
brandy

Cream together hazelnuts, instant coffee or chocolate powder, ricotta cheese and sugar. Whip cream till stiff, then fold into nut cream. Season to taste with brandy, rum or cherry brandy. Pile cream loosely into a glass dish and refrigerate. Serve with cookies and coffee or hot chocolate.

MENU

Chicken Soup with Tapioca
Dumplings (bottom, right)
Swabian Veal Birds with
Spaetzle and Tossed Green Salad (top)
Blueberry Cream (bottom, left)
(pictured Page 72)

Hearty, Distinguished
White or
Velvety Red Wine

Chicken Soup with Tapioca Dumplings

Ingredients for 4 servings:
1 canned, cooked chicken
2 cups chicken broth (cubes)

1/2 cup milk
4 tablespoons butter or margarine
1/2 teaspoon salt
nutmeg
1/3 cup tapioca
1 tablespoon parsley or chervil,
finely chopped
1 egg
2 green peppers
1 onion
1 tablespoon butter

Skin and bone the canned chicken. Combine skin, bones and the jellied can liquid in a saucepan, add 2 cups water and boil for 10 minutes. In the meantime, cut chicken meat in large cubes a little over 1 inch. Bring to a boil the milk with the butter or margarine, salt and nutmeg. Stir in the tapioca, let swell for 2 minutes and add parsley or chervil; stir in the beaten egg. Quarter peppers, remove seeds. Peel onions. Cut peppers and onions in strips. Sauté in butter till transparent. Strain chicken broth into another kettle and add pepper and onion strips. Cook for 10 minutes. With a teaspoon, cut small dumplings from the tapioca mush and drop into the hot broth. Simmer over very low heat till dumplings float to surface.

Swabian Veal Birds with Spaetzle and Tossed Green Salad

Hard-boil eggs, peel and quarter. Flatten veal cutlets with mallet and season. Combine pork sausage, cream and nutmeg and spread this mixture over veal cutlets. Top each cutlet with ¼ of an hard-boiled egg, roll up and secure with toothpicks or wooden skewers. Wash and prepare mushrooms and cut in thin slices. Peel onion and chop finely. Quickly brown veal rolls on all sides in the hot oil and remove from skillet. Sauté diced bacon and chopped onions in the drippings till light yellow. Add tomato paste. Stir for 1 minute. Dust with flour and sauté till flour is lightly browned; add white wine and broth. Add veal rolls and mushrooms and braise for 50 minutes. Transfer veal rolls to serving dish, add some cream to the sauce, season to taste and pour over veal rolls. Serve with spaetzle (next recipe) and tossed green salad which contains water cress.

Ingredients for 4 servings:
2 eggs
8 thin veal chops, 50 g (1³/₄ oz) each
salt
ground, white pepper
4 small pork link sausages
4 tablespoons heavy cream
some nutmeg
250 g (½ lb, plus) fresh mushrooms
1 onion
1 tablespoon oil
1 strip smoked bacon, cubed
1 teaspoon tomato paste
2½ teaspoons flour
½ cup white wine
1 cup meat broth

Spaetzle

Sift flour into a bowl, combine with salt, nutmeg, eggs and warm water, making a dough. Let stand for 15 minutes. Moisten a board with water and spread the spaetzle dough out on it. Then, with a wide knife or scraper, quickly cut off very narrow strips, flinging them right into the boiling water. Simmer spaetzle till they float to surface, then scoop them out with a slotted spoon and keep warm. Repeat till all the dough is used up.

Ingredients for 4 servings:
2¹/₃ cups flour
1 teaspoon salt
pinch nutmeg
4 eggs
1 cup warm water

Blueberry Cream

In a saucepan, combine water, frozen blueberries and sugar and boil for 2 minutes. When blueberries are thawed, force them through a strainer or purée in blender, add cream of wheat and boil for 2 minutes stirring constantly. Turn out into a bowl, add the juice from ½ lemon and beat with mixer or rotary beater for approx. 10 minutes till mixture is frothy. Chill and serve with wafers.

Ingredients for 4 servings:
225 g (8 oz) frozen blueberries
1 cup water
3¹/₂ tablespoons sugar
3 tablespoons cream of wheat
juice from ½ lemon

MENU

Smoked Fillets of Trout (or smoked salmon) (bottom, right)
Rolled Turkey Roast (top)
Corn Stuffed Tomatoes with Figs
Pineapple Surprise (bottom, left)
(pictured Page 73)

Celebrated, Elegant
White Wine

Smoked Fillets of Trout

Ingredients for 4 servings:
4 smoked trout (or salmon slices)
1 grapefruit
1 tablespoon prepared horseradish
2 tablespoons yogurt
juice from ¼ lemon
1 hard-boiled egg
tomato sections
1 lemon
some caviar

Bone and skin the smoked trout. (If you use salmon slices, roll them up). Make a deep saw-tooth score around middle of grapefruit, pull grapefruit apart and squeeze out the juice. Fill one grapefruit half with mixture of prepared horseradish, yogurt and lemon juice. Place in center of platter and arrange smoked trout fillets (or salmon rolls) around it. Garnish with slices of hard-boiled egg, tomato sections and lemon slices. Dot each lemon slice with 1 teaspoon caviar. Serve with toast and butter curls.

Rolled Turkey Roast
with Corn Stuffed Tomatoes and Figs

Ingredients for 4 servings:
1 kg (2¼ lb) boneless rolled turkey
or equal amount of turkey thighs
4 tablespoons oil
1 level teaspoon paprika
salt
some red wine
some meat broth (cubes)
8 tomatoes
1 can (12 oz) whole kernel corn
½ teaspoon paprika
½ cup sour cream
2 level teaspoons corn starch
15 oz canned figs in syrup
¼ cup white wine

Combine 2 tablespoons oil, paprika and salt and roll the meat in this mixture. Heat remaining oil in frying pan and brown meat in it on all sides. Roast, uncovered, in preheated oven at 200°C (390°F) for 1¾ hours, basting repeatedly. After 50 minutes, add some red wine and cover with aluminum foil. When meat is done, remove it from frying pan, place on cutting board, cover and let settle for 10 minutes, then slice. In the meantime, add some meat broth and red wine to pan juices ans boil thoroughly. Cut tops off tomatoes and scoop out pulp. Place tomatoes in shallow saucepan with a little water in it and steam for approx. 3 minutes. Sprinkle with salt. Heat corn, adding paprika. Beat together sour cream and corn starch, add to corn and boil up. Spoon this mixture into the hollow tomatoes. Drain figs, heat in white wine, do not boil, and arrange them around turkey with the stuffed tomatoes. Strain sauce into sauceboat. Serve French fries or mashed potatoes as side dish.

Pineapple Surprise

Cut pineapple in half lengthwise and scoop out the fruit pulp. Refrigerate the two half shells. Cut fruit pulp in fine strips, eliminating all hard and fibrous parts. Combine pineapple strips and cherry preserves, season to taste with rum and spoon mixture into a glass pitcher; chill. Fill pineapple half shells with ice cream and place in freezer for 1 hour. Beat egg whites till stiff, adding a little salt. Add sugar and beat till meringue stands up in soft peaks. Spoon meringue over ice cream in pineapple shells, covering it completely. Dust with powdered sugar and place in preheated oven at 250°C (480°F) till meringue is just light yellow on top. Serve immediately with the chilled pineapple-cherry sauce.

Ingredients for 4 servings:
1 fresh pineapple
6 tablespoons cherry preserves
1 jigger rum
1 pint ice cream (vanilla, strawberry or cherry)
3 egg whites
1 pinch salt
5 tablespoons sugar
some powdered sugar

MENU

Fancy Ham Roll-Ups
Carp, Hungarian Style
Orange Soufflé
(not pictured)

Hearty White Wine

Fancy Ham Roll-Ups

Drain asparagus and divide spears in 8 even portions which you place on the 8 ham slices. Combine oil, garlic powder and cayenne pepper and spoon equal amounts of this dressing over asparagus spears. Then roll ham slices around asparagus spears and serve on platter garnished with egg slices, gherkins and olives.

Ingredients for 4 servings:
500 g (1 lb, plus) white or light green canned asparagus
oil, garlic powder
cayenne pepper
8 slices cooked ham

Carp, Hungarian Style

Wash carp and sprinkle with lemon juice and salt inside and out. Cut smoked bacon into strips and cube onion. Sauté bacon strips briefly in a heavy skillet. Add cubed onion and sauté till yellow. Add the carp and the meat broth, sprinkle carp with pepper, cover and bake in oven at 180°C (375°F) for 30 minutes. Remove lid. Stir together cream and paprika and pour into sauce, stirring well. Baste carp with this sauce several times and bake for 10 more minutes. Serve with roasted potatoes.

Ingredients for 4 servings:
1 carp (approx. 1200 g or 2 lb, 11 oz), ready to cook
juice from 1 lemon
salt
6 strips smoked bacon
2 onions
1/4 cup meat broth
pepper
1 cup sour cream
1 tablespoon paprika

Orange Soufflé

Ingredients for 4 servings:
4 eggs
$^{1}/_{2}$ cup sugar
1 vanilla pod
3 tablespoons flour
1 cup milk
2 tablespoons butter
4 jiggers orange liqueur
8 to 10 ladyfingers
powdered sugar

Beat together egg yolk and sugar. Scoop pulp out of vanilla pod and add to egg yolk cream, then add flour and mix well. In the meantime, bring milk to a boil, take from heat and stir into the creamy mixture. Pour mixture back into saucepan and bring to a boil once more, stirring constantly. Add butter and 2 jiggers orange liqueur. Pour remaining liqueur over ladyfingers. Beat egg whites to a stiff meringue, adding a pinch of salt, and fold this meringue carefully into the warm cream. Grease a fireproof dish and sprinkle with sugar. Spoon approx. half of the cream into the dish, top with the soaked ladyfingers and pour rest of cream over them. Bake soufflé on center rack of preheated oven at 180°C (375°F) for 25 minutes. Remove from oven, dust with powdered sugar and serve immediately.

MENU

Watercress Soup (bottom, left)
Smoked Pork Loin with Variety
Potato Salad (top)
Rum Bananas (bottom, right)
(pictured on opposite Page)

Beer or a Tasty White Wine

Watercress Soup

Ingredients for 4 servings:
125 g ($^{1}/_{4}$ lb) watercress
$^{1}/_{2}$ cup heavy cream
1 egg yolk
1 can (10$^{1}/_{2}$ oz) cream of mushroom soup
some nutmeg

Wash watercress; combine with cream and egg yolk and chop in blender. Cook cream of mushroom soup according to directions and stir the chopped watercress combination into the soup; heat but do not bring to a boil. Season to taste with nutmeg.

Smoked Pork Loin with Variety Potato Salad

Ingredients for 4 servings:
1 kg (2 1/4 lb) smoked pork loin
1 onion; 2 cloves
1 bay leaf
1/2 teaspoon juniper berries
1/2 teaspoon caraway seeds
1 tablespoon grated horseradish
Salad:
7 medium potatoes, boiled in their
jackets
4 pickles; 1 onion
2 hard-boiled eggs
1 tablespoon prepared mustard
vinegar, salt, pepper
2/3 cup plain yogurt

Place smoked pork loin in boiling water. Stud onion with cloves and bay leaf and add to meat in kettle, along with juniper berries and caraway seeds. Cover and simmer for approx. 40 minutes; do not boil. Peel and slice potatoes, slice pickles. Peel onion, chop finely. Peel and cube eggs. Mix all these ingredients and season to taste with the above seasonings and stir in the yogurt.

Rum Bananas

Ingredients for 4 servings:
4 bananas
4 tablespoons apricot jam
2 jiggers rum
some grated chocolate
and some maraschino cherries

Slit banana peels in center lengthwise; remove and discard 1/2 peel from each banana. Carefully lift bananas out of remaining peel halves and cut each banana into diagonal slices. Stir together apricot jam and rum and distribute among the 4 empty peel halves. Return banana slices to peel halves, arranging them over jam in their original order. Sprinkle each serving with grated chocolate and garnish with maraschino cherries.

MENU

Meat Broth with Crepe Chips
Viennese Deep Fried Chicken
with Lettuce Hearts and Herbed
Sour Cream
Vanilla Ice Cream with Pineapple
Rings and Hot Cherry Sauce
(not pictured)

Fruity, Tasty White Wine

Meat Broth with Crepe Chips

Ingredients for 4 servings:
3 1/2 tablespoons flour
1 cup milk
1 egg
pinch salt
some butter
5 cups strong meat broth or stock

In a dish, combine flour and milk and beat egg into this mixture, making a thin pancake batter. Add some salt and set aside for 30 minutes. Melt butter in skillet or omelet pan, then pour in the batter, a small quantity at a time, and make very thin pancakes which you turn out on a board for cooling. It is all right to let them dry out a little in the process. Heat meat broth, cut pancakes into squares and place them in a soup tureen. Pour the hot broth over them and serve soup immediately.

Viennese Deep Fried Chicken

Quarter and bone chickens. Season meat with salt and pepper and let stand for a few minutes. Turn meat first in flour, then in beaten egg and last in bread crumbs into which the paprika has been mixed. Each piece must be thickly coated. Heat shortening to 175°C (350°F) and deep fry chicken pieces in it for 15 minutes. Drain and serve on a platter lined with paper napkins. Serve French fries as a side dish.

Ingredients for 4 servings:
2 chickens, approx. 750 g (1 1/2 lb) each
pepper, salt, flour
1 to 2 eggs
bread crumbs
1/2 teaspoon paprika
shortening for deep frying

Lettuce Hearts in Herbed Sour Cream

Combine cream, lemon juice and orange juice. Season to taste with the chopped herbs, salt, sugar, freshly ground pepper and prepared mustard. Remove the outer, darker leaves from lettuce heads. Wash lettuce hearts, drain well and serve whole with the herbed sour cream poured over them.

Ingredients for 4 servings:
1/2 cup sour cream
juice from 1 lemon and 1/2 orange
1 tablespoon chopped herbs (parsley, chervil, tarragon, dill)
some salt and sugar
pepper
prepared mustard
2 heads butter lettuce

Vanilla Ice Cream with Pineapple Rings and Hot Cherry Sauce

Drain cherries, reserving syrup. Combine syrup with sugar and bring to a boil. Dissolve corn starch in some cold water and add to the hot syrup. Bring to a boil and cook briefly, stirring constantly. Then, add cherry brandy and cherries. Place 2 scoops vanilla ice cream into each serving dish, top with a pineapple ring, and pour the hot cherry sauce around ice cream. Serve immediately.

Ingredients for 4 servings:
1 can (16 oz) tart cherries
1 to 2 tablespoons sugar
1 to 2 teaspoons corn starch
2 jiggers cherry brandy
4 pineapple rings
8 scoops vanilla ice cream

MENU

Clear Meat Broth with Cheese
Floats (bottom, right)
Veal Shanks with Vegetables
in "Bird Nests" (top)
Wine Jelly (bottom, left)
(pictured Page 81)

Hearty, Distinguished
Red Wine

Clear Meat Broth with Cheese Floats

Ingredients for 4 servings:
2 eggs
pinch salt
2 tablespoons flour
1/4 teaspoon baking
powder
1/2 cup grated cheese
some paprika
4 cups clear meat broth

Add a little salt to egg whites and beat till stiff. In a bowl, combine flour, baking powder and grated cheese, reserving 1 tablespoon of the grated cheese. Fold beaten egg yolks and flour mixture into meringue. Line a baking sheet with wax paper and spread cheese mixture on it in a 3/8-inch layer. Sprinkle with paprika and cheese and bake immediately in preheated oven at 220°C (430°F) for 10 minutes till golden yellow. Let cool and cut in diamond shapes which you float on the hot broth. Sprinkle with chopped parsley if desired.

Veal Shanks with Vegetables in "Bird Nests"

Ingredients for 4 servings:
1 veal shank approx.
1 1/2 kg (3 1/2 lb)
salt, pepper
1 onion
1 carrot
2 tablespoons oil
1 tablespoon tomato paste
1/4 teaspoon basil or
tarragon
1 level teaspoon corn starch
1 cup water
750 g (1 1/2 lb, plus) new green
beans
2 tablespoons butter
4 tomatoes
1 pkg whole, frozen carrots (10 oz)
1 teaspoon sugar
1 pkg frozen green peas (10 oz)
1 tablespoon chopped chervil

Season veal shank with salt and pepper. Heat oil in frying pan, add veal shank and roast in preheated oven at 200°C (390°F) for 25 minutes. Add the diced onion and carrot, cover and braise for at least one more hour, turning twice. Remove veal shank from pan and add tomato paste, basil or tarragon and 1 cup water to pan drippings and bring to a boil. Thicken sauce with corn starch and strain. Cook beans in salted water, drain and pour browned butter over them. Cut a cross into each tomato, sprinkle with oil and salt and place under broiler for 8 minutes. Cook carrots and peas according to package directions, drain and season to taste with salt and sugar, adding some fresh butter. "Bird Nests": Peel potatoes and cut in long, thin strips. Place portions of these "shoestring potatoes" in a bird nest spoon (available at gourmet stores), fry in deep fat and release from spoon when they are golden brown.
Fill one half of the bird nests with carrots, the other half with peas. Sprinkle carrots in nests with chopped chervil. Arrange nests around veal shank on serving plate, alternating them with the broiled tomatoes.

80

Wine Jelly

Ingredients for 4 servings:
1 can (16 oz) fruit cocktail
1/2 cup white wine
juice from 1/2 lemon
1 teaspoon vanilla
1 tablespoon sugar
2 jiggers fruit liqueur
1 envelope unflavored gelatine

Soften gelatine in 5 tablespoons cold water for 5 minutes. Pour 1/4 cup of the fruit syrup in a small saucepan, add the softened gelatine and stir over low heat till dissolved. Add remaining fruit syrup, white wine, lemon juice, sugar, vanilla and fruit liqueur. Distribute canned fruits among 4 serving dishes and pour the fruit syrup with the gelatine over them. Refrigerate till firm. Note: If a clear wine jelly is desired, omit the fruit.

MENU

Grapefruits "Camarones"
(background and foreground)
Loin Roast with Vegetables (center)
Chocolate Cream Dessert
(front, right)
(pictured on front cover)

Rosé Champagne

Grapefruits "Camarones"

Ingredients for 4 servings:
4 grapefruits
250 g (1 lb, plus) cooked shrimps
1 can (4 oz) sliced mushrooms
3 tablespoons tomato ketchup
3 tablespoons chili sauce
1 1/4 tablespoon grated horseradish, fresh or prepared;
juice from 1/4 lemon
2 tablespoons mayonnaise

Cut tops of grapefruits, forming saw-tooth edges. Scrape out fruit pulp and white fibers. If shrimps are frozen, thaw according to directions; if canned, drain. Mix the prepared shrimps with the drained mushroom slices and spoon into grapefruit shells. Make a cocktail sauce by combining ketchup, chili sauce, horseradish, lemon juice and mayonnaise and pour sauce over shrimps. Serve with toast and butter curls.

Loin Roast with Vegetables

Remove membrane from loin roast. If desired, lard loin roast with strips of bacon. Season with salt and pepper. Preheat oven to 225°C (440°F) and heat oil in frying pan. Quickly brown the loin roast in the hot oil on all sides, then roast meat for 25 to 30 minutes till done. After the first 10 minutes, add the cubed onion. When meat is done, remove it from frying pan and keep warm for 10 minutes. In the meantime, add broth to pan drippings and thicken with corn starch which has been dissolved in the white wine. Strain sauce and season to taste. If desired, add 2 tablespoons heavy cream. Cut roast in slices and serve with vegetables on platter. Side dishes: French fries or potato croquettes (recipe on Page 59).

Ingredients for 4 servings:
750 g (1 ½ lb, plus) beef loin roast
salt, pepper
2 tablespoons oil
1 onion
1 tablespoon butter
1 cup chicken broth (cubes)
1 teaspoon corn starch
3 tablespoons white wine

Chocolate Cream Dessert

In top of double boiler, stir together egg yolks and sugar. Add chocolate, cocoa, instant coffee powder and cinnamon. Pour the hot milk over it all and beat over boiling water for 2 to 3 minutes. Soften gelatine in 5 tablespoons cold water for 5 minutes, then dissolve it in the hot cream in top of double boiler, stirring constantly. Refrigerate chocolate cream till it just begins to set, then fold in the whipped cream to which 1 tablespoon sugar and 1 teaspoon vanilla have been added. Last, stir in rum or brandy to taste. Spoon chocolate cream into individual serving dishes rinsed out with cold water, or pour into a large dish. Refrigerate for approx. 1 to 2 hours. Decorate with candied cherries if desired.

Ingredients for 4 servings:
4 egg yolks
2 tablespoons sugar
3 tablespoons coarsely chopped, plain milk chocolate
1 tablespoon cocoa
1 teaspoon instant coffee powder
pinch cinnamon
1 cup hot milk
2 teaspoons unflavored gelatine
1 cup heavy cream
1 teaspoon vanilla
1 tablespoon sugar
1 to 2 jiggers rum or brandy

Shrimp-Stuffed Avocados (top, left)
Mixed Grill with Herbed Butter and
Shoestring Potatoes
(top, right)
Cold Melon Soup (bottom)
(pictured on opposite Page)

Fruity White Wine or
Fiery, Full-Bodied Red Wine

Shrimp-Stuffed Avocados

Ingredients for 4 servings:
2 avocados
75 g (2¹/₂ oz) shrimps
75 g (2¹/₂ oz) lobster meat; some
lemon juice; oil
salt, pepper
¹/₂ cup mayonnaise
1 teaspoon prepared mustard
1 teaspoon grated horseradish (fresh
or prepared)
2 tablespoons whipped cream;
1 tablespoon tomato ketchup
1 tablespoon sherry

Cut avocados in half lengthwise, remove seeds. Scoop out fruit pulp, leaving a thin lining in the half shells. Cube pulp and lobster meat, combine with shrimps and refrigerate in a marinade of lemon juice, oil, salt and pepper. Combine mayonnaise, prepared mustard, horseradish, whipped cream and tomato ketchup. Add sherry to taste. Stir the marinated ingredients into this sauce and serve the salad in the 4 avocado half shells.

Mixed Grill with Herbed Butter and Shoestring Potatoes

Ingredients for 4 servings:
4 tablespoons butter
1 tablespoon chopped
parsley, chervil or watercress
¹/₂ teaspoon lemon juice
some salt (only if butter is not
salted)
pepper
4 slices filet mignon beef, 75 g (2¹/₂
oz) each
4 veal loin cutlets, 75 g (2¹/₂ oz)
each
4 slices veal or beef kidneys
2 Frankfurters or Wieners
2 slices bacon
For the shoestring potatoes:
4 large potatoes; shortening for
deep-frying
salt

Cream the butter. Wash herbs, drain, chop finely and mix with lemon juice, salt, pepper and the creamed butter. Roll the herbed butter in a sheet of wax paper, forming a round log. Twist ends of paper and place butter roll in freezer. Season meat and kidneys with pepper. Cut Frankfurters or Wieners and the bacon slices in half crosswise. Broil bacon slices in a preheated broil pan (with grooved bottom) for ¹/₂ minute. Add veal cutlets and Frankfurter halves and pan-broil for 4 minutes, turning once. Remove from pan and keep warm. Pan-broil filet mignon steaks and kidney slices for 4 minutes, turning once. Sprinkle all meat with a little salt and serve immediately with slices from the chilled, herbed butter roll. For the shoestring potatoes, peel the potatoes and cut in very thin slices (by hand or with a vegetable slicer). Place slices on a board and cut them in long, thin strips. Rinse, drain and fry in deep fat till crisp. Note: To save time, purchase frozen, ready-to-cook shoestring potatoes from your supermarket.

Cold Melon Soup

Ingredients for 4 servings:
1 to 2 honeydew melons
2 cups red wine
2 tablespoons tapioca
4 to 5 tablespoons sugar
juice from 2 lemons
1 cup club soda

In saucepan, combine red wine, tapioca and sugar. Bring to a boil and simmer for 10 minutes. Set aside to cool. Cut melons in half, remove seeds and cut enough small melon balls from pulp to fill 2 cups. Force remaining pulp through a sieve or puree in blender. Stir melon puree, lemon juice and club soda into the cooled wine soup. Add melon balls. Season to taste and serve in glass dishes or soup bowls.

MENU

Stuffed Eggs with Smoked Salmon and Caviar
Roast Chicken in White Wine Sauce
Strawberries in Burgundy
(not pictured)

Tasty White Wine

Stuffed Eggs with Smoked Salmon and Caviar

Ingredients for 4 servings:
6 eggs
1 tablespoon tomato paste
1 tablespoon butter
some onion and garlic powder
1 tablespoon mayonnaise
1 tablespoon fresh, finely chopped red and green pepper
1/2 tablespoon chopped parsley
approx. 10 slices smoked salmon
4 tablespoons caviar

Place eggs in warm water, bring to a boil and boil for 8 minutes. Rinse eggs with cold water, peel and cut in half lengthwise. Scoop out yolks. Cream 3 of the yolks with tomato paste and softened butter and some onion or garlic powder. Cream the 3 remaining egg yolks with the mayonnaise, then add the chopped peppers and parsley. Squirt the creamed egg yolk combinations into the egg white halves, using a pastry tube, and arrange the stuffed eggs on a platter. Serve with caviar and slices of smoked salmon; garnish with onion rings. Have fresh toast slices and butter curls ready to go along.

Roast Chicken in White Wine Sauce

Quarter chicken and rub with salt and pepper. Heat butter and oil in saucepan and brown chicken parts briefly in the hot fat on all sides, approx. 5 minutes, till light yellow. Remove chicken parts from pan. Wash, clean and chop the green onions. Dice bacon. Place both ingredients in saucepan and sauté till transparent, stirring constantly. Grate garlic clove and add to pan. Add cognac, ignite and burn off. After flames have died down, dust contents of pan with flour and sauté till just yellow. Fill up with wine and return chicken parts to saucepan. Add meat broth, bay leaf and thyme and simmer for approx. 40 minutes. Remove meat pieces from saucepan and keep warm. Add cream to liquid and bring to a boil again, cooking for another 4 to 5 minutes with lid removed. Wash, prepare and slice the mushrooms. Heat butter and sauté mushrooms in it for 2 minutes. Add salt and pepper. Add mushrooms to chicken sauce, return chicken parts to saucepan and cook for another 4 minutes.

Ingredients for 4 servings:
1 roasting chicken, ready to cook (approx. 1 1/2 kg or 3 1/2 lb)
salt, pepper
5 tablespoons butter
4 tablespoons oil
6 green onions
4 strips smoked bacon
2 cloves garlic
1/4 cup cognac or aged brandy
1 1/4 tablespoons flour
3 cups dry white wine (preferably Riesling)
2 tablespoons meat broth
1/2 bay leaf
250 g (1/2 lb, plus) fresh mushrooms
1 tablespoon butter
salt, pepper
1/4 teaspoon thyme
1 cup heavy cream

Strawberries in Burgundy

Rinse strawberries individually under cold running water, holding them by their stems. Gently remove stems and caps and distribute strawberries over 4 servings dishes. Dust each serving with 1 teaspoon powdered sugar and cover with clear plastic. Refrigerate for approx. 1 hour. Chill red Burgundy or champagne till very cold. Place the chilled strawberries on a tray and pour some cold Burgundy or champagne over each serving. Serve immediately with ladyfingers.

Ingredients for 4 servings:
500 g (1 lb, plus) fresh strawberries
4 tablespoons powdered sugar
3 cups red Burgundy or red champagne

MENU

Corn Kernel Soup (top, left)
Pork Crown Roast (bottom)
Apricots Flambée (top, right)
(pictured on Page 89)

Hearty White Wine, Light Red Wine
or Rosé

Corn Kernel Soup

Ingredients for 4 servings:
1 onion; 1 carrot
2 medium potatoes
1 green pepper
4 strips smoked bacon
1 tablespoon flour
3 cups water
bouillon concentrate (cubes or
granules) for 2 cups liquid
1 can (12 oz) whole kernel corn;
1 cup milk
some ground, white pepper
1 tablespoon chopped parsley

Peel onion, carrot and potatoes. Quarter pepper pod and
remove seeds. Chop these ingredients and the bacon.
Sauté chopped bacon briefly in a saucepan, add the chopped
vegetables and sauté in bacon drippings for approx. 3 minutes. Dust with flour, add 3 cups water and the bouillon concentrate. Cook soup for 25 minutes, then add corn kernels
with their liquid, and the milk. Heat, do not boil. Sprinkle
with pepper and chopped parsley. Serve with French bread.

Pork Crown Roast

Ingredients for 4 servings:
1 lean pork crown roast section
with 10 to 12 ribs (have butcher
remove backbone)
2 teaspoons sage
1 teaspoon thyme
1/2 teaspoon ground caraway
some salt and pepper
3 tablespoons oil
1 onion
1 carrot
1 cup white wine
1/2 cup heavy cream
1 1/4 teaspoon corn starch

Have butcher shape crown roast and tie it securely once
around loin area and once near bone tips, or shape the crown
yourself and sew ends together with twine; remove meat from
top inch of each rib so bone tips will show. Season and oil
meat. Place meat in frying pan with oil and surround it with
the chopped carrots and onions. Preheat oven to 200°C
(390°F) and roast meat for approx. 1 1/2 hours. Remove meat
from pan and add white wine to pan drippings, boil thoroughly
and strain. Beat together cream and corn starch and thicken
sauce with this mixture. Serve pork crown roast on platter.
Bone points may be decorated with grapes or cherries. Suitable side dishes are: Mashed potatoes, steamed red cabbage
(commercially available in jars – or prepare from basic recipe
on Page 59), pear halves filled with cranberries, a mixed salad
platter, Brussels sprouts, mushrooms, green beans, potato
croquettes (recipe on Page 59), and apple sauce.

Apricots Flambée

Ingredients for 4 servings:
750 g (1 1/2 lb, plus) firm, ripe
apricots
1 tablespoon butter
1 teaspoon sugar
3 tablespoons apricot jam
1/4 cup flaming brandy
1/2 cup white wine
8 scoops vanilla ice cream

Wash, drain and halve apricots; remove seeds. Place an enameled skillet or a copper skillet over a table burner. Heat butter and sugar in skillet till yellow. Add apricots and apricot jam and sauté for 1 minute. Pour the flaming brandy over it all, ignite and burn off. Add white wine and cook for another 3 to 4 minutes. Distribute vanilla ice cream among 4 serving dishes, top with the hot apricots and serve immediately. Note: The apricots will acquire a uniquely tart flavor if a few inner kernels from cracked apricot seeds are cooked along with them.

MENU

*Asparagus Cocktail
"Spring Evening" (bottom, left)
Sukiyaki (top)
Peaches with Blackberry Sauce
(bottom, right)
(pictured on Page 92)*

Beer

Asparagus Cocktail "Spring Evening"

Ingredients for 2 servings:
300 g (10 1/2 oz) canned, white or
light green asparagus
salt, sugar
2 cups frozen shrimps
4 tablespoons heavy cream
3 tablespoons tomato ketchup
dash brandy
1 tablespoon lemon juice
some paprika or cayenne pepper
2 tablespoons pineapple chunks
1 hard-boiled egg
2 lettuce leaves

Drain asparagus spears and cut in 2-inch sections. Thaw shrimps. For cocktail sauce, whip cream and mix with tomato ketchup, brandy, lemon juice and paprika or cayenne pepper. Wash and drain lettuce leaves and line 2 refrigerated cocktail glasses with them. Arrange asparagus pieces, shrimps and pineapple chunks over them. Pour some of the cocktail sauce over each serving and sprinkle with crushed ice. Serve with crisp toast slices and sweet butter curls.

Sukiyaki

Preparations in the kitchen: Remove membrane and gristle from meat and cut meat in thin slivers approx. 1/2 cm (under 1/4 inch). (It is easier to sliver meat when it is partially frozen). Arrange meat slivers attractively on a platter and cover with foil. Wash and prepare vegetables and cut in thin strips. Arrange vegetable strips on a platter and cover with foil also. Cut butter with a ripple knife and arrange the decorative butter slices on a glass plate. Cook rice. Set the table for sukiyaki, providing for each guest a beer glass, a soup bowl or soup cup, and a fork. Also, set out dishes for the egg shells since eggs will be broken at table, and for the egg whites (which will not be used). Have a table burner with a skillet ready, also a large fork for transferring meat slices. Further, have available some sugar, soy sauce, red wine or sherry, eggs, salt and pepper. Pour the cold beer and serve the rice.

Now, the cooking at the table begins. Heat skillet and melt butter in it. Add 1 teaspoon sugar and stir till it turns light yellow. Pour on 1/4 cup soy sauce and 1/4 cup red wine or sherry and add one half of the prepared vegetables. Sauté while stirring frequently. Push vegetables to one side of skillet and place one half of the meat slivers in skillet. Boil up briefly and season with salt and pepper. Break and separate eggs, sliding 1 egg yolk into each serving bowl. Spoon the cooked vegetables and meat over egg yolk and mix. This Asiatic feast will be even more genuine if you also use water chestnuts, bean sprouts, bamboo sprouts and mushrooms and replace the rice with Chinese noodles (bean threads) which are cooked at table along with the vegetables and meat.

Ingredients for 2 servings:
190 g (6 1/2 oz) filet mignon
190 g (6 1/2 oz) veal tenderloin
500 g (1 lb, plus) fresh vegetables (1 onion, 1 carrot, 1/2 head cauliflower, 1/4 head cabbage, zuccini, some fresh spinach or watercress, onion rings)
2 tablespoons butter
some sugar and soy sauce
1/4 cup red wine or sherry
2 eggs
salt, pepper

Peaches with Blackberry Sauce

Dip peaches briefly in hot water, then peel, halve and remove seeds. In a shallow saucepan, heat 1 cup water and the sugar. Steam peach halves in this syrup for 5 minutes and lift out with slotted spoon. Add blackberries to syrup and boil up. Add vanilla and remove saucepan from heat. Allow sauce to cool, then stir in liqueur, rum, the cherry brandy or brandy and some lemon juice to taste. Place peaches in glass serving dishes, cavities up. Whip cream, adding a little sugar, and squirt it into peach halves from a pastry tube. Sprinkle with toasted almond slivers and serve with blackberry sauce.

Ingredients for 2 servings:
2 fresh peaches
2 1/4 tablespoons sugar
1 teaspoon vanilla
60 g (2 oz) blackberries
1 jigger red fruit liqueur
some rum, cherry brandy or brandy
juice from 1/2 lemon
1/4 cup heavy cream
1 tablespoon almond slivers

MENU

Lobster Salad
Stuffed Veal Cutlets
Potato Swirls
Mixed Vegetable Side Dish
Champagne Sherbet
(pictured on Page 93)

Celebrated White Wine

Lobster Salad

Ingredients for 4 servings:
200 g (7 oz) lobster or crab meat
1 pkg (10 oz) mixed,
frozen vegetables
some paprika
2 teaspoons tomato ketchup
lettuce leaves
lemon
toast
butter

Flake lobster or crab meat and combine with vegetables. Add paprika and ketchup to taste and serve on lettuce leaves in individual serving dishes. Decorate with lemon slices and serve with crisp toast triangles and butter curls.

Stuffed Veal Cutlets

Ingredients for 4 servings:
1 veal tenderloin (approx, 600 g or 21 oz)
125 g (1/2 lb) ground veal
1 can (4 oz) sliced mushrooms
1 teaspoon brandy or sherry
salt, pepper, flour; 1 egg
3 tablespoons slivered almonds
2 tablespoons bread crumbs
1 tablespoon butter or margarine
1 envelope brown gravy mix
2 tablespoons sour cream

Skin the veal loin and cut it in 8 equal slices. Flatten slices lightly with a mallet and cut a pocket in each. Combine ground veal, sliced mushrooms and brandy, stuff cutlets with this mixture and secure openings with wooden skewers. Season cutlets and dip first in flour, then in beaten egg, and last in a mixture of slivered almonds and bread crumbs. Fry in the hot fat for approx. 15 minutes, turning once. Serve on a warm platter. Mix the brown gravy according to package directions, using the juice from the canned mushrooms and adding enough water to come up with the required amount of liquid. Add 2 tablespoons sour cream. Combine gravy mixture with pan drippings, boil up and stir.

94

Potato Swirls

Prepare 4 servings of instant mashed potatoes according to package directions. Add nutmeg and stir in the beaten egg. Fill this mixture into a pastry tube with a star tip and squirt onto a greased baking sheet, forming rings. Brush with the beaten egg yolk and bake in oven at 180°C (375°F) for approx. 10 minutes. Dust potato swirls with a little paprika if desired.

Ingredients for 4 servings:
Instant mashed potatoes
for 4 servings
plus the required amount of salt,
butter, water and milk
some nutmeg
1 egg
1 egg yolk

Mixed Vegetable Side Dish

In a saucepan, combine the canned asparagus and artichoke bottoms, heat but do not boil. Combine frozen vegetables, fat and some of the liquid from the artichoke bottoms, add salt and sugar and steam till done. Arrange asparagus spears beside meat on serving platter and stick some into centers of potato swirls. Arrange carrots and peas on opposite side of serving platter.

Ingredients for 4 servings:
1 can (11 oz) white or light green
asparagus
14 oz artichoke bottoms, canned
1 pkg frozen peas and carrots
(10 oz)
1 tablespoon butter or margarine
salt
pinch sugar

Champagne Sherbet

Whip cream with 1 tablespoon sugar and the vanilla till it stands up in soft peaks. Add remaining sugar and fold in the champagne and the lemon juice. Place in freezer for several hours, stirring once or twice. When sherbet is frozen, spoon it into serving dishes and decorate with cherries and wafers or ladyfingers.

Ingredients for 4 servings:
1 1/2 cups heavy cream
1 teaspoon vanilla
3 tablespoons sugar
1 cup champagne
juice from 1/4 lemon
4 cherries
ladyfingers or wafers

MENU

Stuffed Eggs with Herbed Cream
Frenched Veal Rib Roast
with Tomatoes and Chicory
Peach Tartlets
(pictured on oppos. Page)

___

Distinguished
White Wine

Stuffed Eggs with Herbed Cream

Ingredients for 4 servings:
4 hard-boiled eggs
1 tablespoon butter or margarine
1 teaspoon prepared mustard
salt, monosodium glutamate
1 cup sour cream
1 tablespoon chopped green herbs
1/4 lemon
some paprika

Peel eggs and cut in half lengthwise. Remove egg yolks and mash with fork. Combine the soft butter or margarine with mustard, salt and monosodium glutamate and squirt this mixture into the egg halves, then stick them back together with pointed ends far apart, as shown on opposite page. Arrange stuffed eggs on a platter, open ends up, and pour the herbed cream sauce around them. This sauce is mixed from sour cream and chopped herbs of your choice, with lemon juice and salt added to taste. Sprinkle egg tops with paprika.

Frenched Veal Rib Roast with Tomatoes and Chicory

Ingredients for 4 servings:

1 kg (2 1/4 lb) veal rib roast
salt, pepper, thyme
3 tablespoons oil
1 cup chopped onion, root celery
and carrot – mixed
1/2 cup white wine
1/2 of a 28-oz can peeled tomatoes
4 chicories
1/2 lemon
2 tablespoons oil
1 tablespoon butter
or margarine

Remove meat from top inch of each rib so bone tips will show. Season meat with salt, pepper and thyme and brown in the hot oil on all sides. Roast in frying pan in oven at 200°C (390°F) for 1 hour and 15 minutes. After the first 10 minutes, add the chopped vegetables. When meat is done, remove it from pan and keep warm. Add white wine and a little water to pan juices and boil till baked-on residues dissolve. Add the liquid from the canned tomatoes, boil up, stir and remove from heat; strain. Serve this sauce separately in a sauce boat. Decorate bone tips with paper frills. Preparation of vegetables to be served on same platter: In a saucepan, combine chicory, 1/2 cup water, lemon juice, oil and salt. Cover and cook over low heat for approx. 25 minutes. Drain chicory well, then sauté it in hot fat in skillet and season with salt and pepper. For another decorative side dish, ripple-cut potato slices, boil them briefly in water, then drain ans fry in deep fat till done. Arrange on serving platter and dust with paprika.

Peach Tartlets

Ingredients for 4 servings:
4 canned peach halves, peeled
4 patty shells or mini tarts (frozen)
2 tablespoons red fruit jam
some cherry brandy
1 pkg (8 oz) cream cheese
$^1/_4$ lemon
1 teaspoon vanilla
3 tablespoons sugar
$^1/_3$ cup milk

Drain peach halves. Bake patty shells or mini tarts and brush on inside with a mixture of jam and cherry brandy. Top each with a peach half, cavities up. Cream together cream cheese, lemon juice, vanilla, sugar and milk. Spoon cream into peach halves and decorate each with a maraschino cherry if desired.

MENU

Chiche Lorraine
Roast Beef with French Fries
and Vegetables
Peaches Flambée
(not pictured)

Rosé Wine

Quiche Lorraine

Ingredients for 4 servings:
1 $^2/_3$ cups flour
$^1/_2$ teaspoon salt
$^1/_2$ cup butter
$^1/_3$ cup plus 2 tablespoons water
250 g ($^1/_2$ lb, plus) Emmental (Swiss) cheese
125 g ($^1/_4$ lb) sliced ham, smoked (Virginia style or prosciutto)
1 tablespoon butter
4 eggs
1 cup heavy cream
$^1/_2$ cup milk
pepper, nutmeg

Sift flour into a bowl, add salt and butter and work these ingredients together with your hands into a crumbly mass. Add water and quickly work everything into a dough. Refrigerate dough for approx. 1 hour. In the meantime, cut cheese in thin slices, sauté ham in butter till just transparent. Roll the refrigerated dough out into a circle about $^1/_4$ inch ($^1/_2$ cm) thick and cover the bottom of an 11-inch (28 cm) spring form with it, allowing for a 1-inch (2 $^1/_2$ cm) turned up edge. Prick dough with fork several times. Arrange cheese and bacon slices over dough. Beat together eggs, cream and milk. Season with pepper and nutmeg and pour over cheese and bacon. Preheat oven to 225°C (440°F) and bake the Quiche Lorraine on lower rack for 30 minutes. Turn out on serving platter and serve immediately.

Roast Beef with French Fries and Vegetables

Season meat with salt and pepper, peel and chop onions. Preheat oven to 225°C (440°F). Brown the beef in the hot fat in frying pan on all sides. Add onions and roast the beef in oven for approx. 25 minutes. Remove to heated platter and let settle for 15 minutes before carving. Add meat broth to pan juices, boil up and thicken with corn starch that has been dissolved in a little cold water. Serve with French fries and assorted cooked vegetables of your choice.

Ingredients for 4 servings:
750 g (1 1/2 lb, plus) roast beef
salt, pepper
2 onions
1 tablespoon shortening
1 cup meat broth (cubes)
1 teaspoon corn starch
(level)

Peaches Flambée

Dip peaches briefly in boiling water, then peel and cut in half, removing seeds. Rub sugar cubes against the oranges till cubes are saturated with the oil from the peels. Place enamel or copper skillet over table burner and heat butter in it till foamy. Add 1 tablespoon sugar and make a golden yellow caramel of the melted butter and sugar. Squeeze oranges. Add orange juice, sugar cubes and peaches and boil till a thick syrup results. Pour on the orange liqueur, ignite and serve with vanilla cream (recipe on Page 142 of Appendix).

Ingredients for 4 servings:
4 ripe, firm peaches
2 oranges
6 sugar cubes
1 tablespoon butter
1 tablespoon sugar
1/2 cup orange liqueur

MENU

Pasties a la Queen
"India" Style Pork Loin Cutlets
with Curry Rice
Chocolate Cream
(pictured on oppos. Page, top)

Hearty White Wine

Pasties à la Queen

Ingredients for 4 servings:
4 patty shells (frozen)
125 g (4 ½ oz) canned ragout fin
(or prepare from basic recipe on
Page 143 of Appendix)
some Worcestershire sauce
4 lemon sections
some parsley

Bake patty shells. Heat ragout fin (or prepare from scratch) and season with Worcestershire sauce. Spoon ragout fin into patty shells and decorate with lemon sections and parsley sprigs.

"India" Style Pork Loin Cutlets

Ingredients for 4 servings:
8 pork loin cutlets
1 teaspoon curry
some salt
2 tablespoons oil
1 cup canned fruits, diced
2 tablespoons slivered
almonds
2 pkgs (at 1 oz or 28,4 g) brown
gravy mix

Season meat with curry and salt and fry till each slice is white all the way through; it must not be pink inside. Remove meat from skillet and spoon the drained, cubed fruits into pan drippings, season with curry and heat thoroughly. Then, spoon over meat on serving platter and sprinkle with toasted almond slivers. Prepare the brown gravy from mix according to package instructions and add a little curry to it.

Curry Rice

Ingredients for 4 servings:
2 cups rice
½ teaspoon curry
2 tablespoons oil
2 cups hot water
1 bay leaf; some salt
dash monosodium glutamate

Combine rice, curry and oil in a saucepan, add the hot water, bay leaf, salt and monosodium glutamate. Cook for 18 minutes, stir and serve.

Chocolate Cream

Ingredients for 4 servings:
2 cups heavy cream
2 teaspoons vanilla
2 tablespoons sugar
4 tablespoons instant chocolate
drink mix
a few drops rum or cherry brandy

Whip cream till it stands up in soft peaks. Carefully fold in sugar, instant chocolate mix and rum or cherry brandy. Refrigerate, decorate in any desired fashion and serve.

100

MENU

Colorful Salads
with Fine Condiments
Pasties with Poached Eggs
Sirloin Steaks with Artichoke
Bottoms
Sauce Béarnaise
Stuffed Tomatoes
Potato Wafers
Apricot Sherbet
(pictured on Page, 101, bottom)

———

Champagne
Full-Bodied Red Wine

Colorful Salads with Fine Condiments

Tuna Salad

Slice tuna chunks and tomatoes and arrange on 4 individual serving plates. Sprinkle all with capers, salt, pepper, vinegar and oil. If desired, dust with onion and garlic powder.

Trimmings:

8 slices salami
8 slices Canadian bacon
2 eggs
4 tablespoons caviar
¹/₄ lemon

Decorate serving plates with salami, Canadian bacon and stuffed eggs. For stuffed eggs, cut hard-boiled eggs in half lengthwise, remove yolks and chop. Place 1 tablespoon caviar in each egg half and sprinkle the chopped egg yolks around edges, as shown on Page 101, bottom. Then, sprinkle the visible peak of each caviar mound with some lemon juice.

Chicken Salad

Ingredients for 4 servings:
1 cup cooked chicken
1 pineapple ring
1 apple
¹/₄ celery root
1 teaspoon Worcestershire sauce
¹/₂ cup heavy cream

Cut chicken, apple and celery root in slices, the pineapple ring in strips. Season with salt and pepper and Worcestershire sauce; combine with unsweetened whipped cream.

Vegetable Salad

Prepare, clean and slice carrot and celery root and steam in a little salted water till done. Set aside to cool, then combine with the green peas, salt, pepper and some lemon juice and oil. Season to taste and refrigerate before serving.

Ingredients for 4 servings:
2 carrots
$^1/_2$ celery root
$^1/_2$ cup cooked green peas
juice from $^1/_2$ lemon

Pasties with Poached Eggs

Bake patty shells according to directions. Cube ham and tomatoes. Sauté the chopped onion and diced bacon in the hot fat till light yellow. Add the crushed garlic clove and $^1/_2$ cup liquid from the canned tomatoes. Cook for 5 minutes and add ham and tomato cubes. Beat together corn starch and cream and stir into sauce. Stir in the chopped herbs and season with salt and pepper to taste. Break eggs into a cup, one at a time, and carefully slide them into the boiling water. Simmer till egg whites become firm. Bake patty shells according to directions. Spoon the vegetable-bacon ragout into the patty shells and top each with a poached egg.

Ingredients for 4 servings:
4 patty shells (frozen)
150 g (5 oz) cooked ham
4 canned, peeled tomatoes
1 onion
4 slices bacon
1 teaspoon butter or margarine
1 clove garlic
$^1/_3$ cup heavy cream
1 teaspoon corn starch
chopped herbs
salt, pepper
4 eggs
some vinegar

Sirloin Steaks with Artichoke Bottoms

Fry steaks in a lightly oiled, heavy skillet on both sides. Total cooking time is 9 to 10 minutes for rare, 11 to 12 minutes for medium and approx. 20 minutes for well-done. Remove from skillet, season with salt and pepper and keep warm. Place artichoke bottoms in steak drippings and heat through quickly. Top steaks on platter with artichoke bottoms. Sauce Béarnaise: In a saucepan, bring to a boil vinegar, white wine, chopped green onions and tarragon and cook till liquid is reduced to one tablespoon. Add egg yolk and beat over boiling water till foamy. Remove from heat and gradually stir in the butter. If sauce curdles, add a tablespoon cold water and carefully beat mixture with a wire whisk, starting at edge of saucepan. Stuffed Tomatoes: Cut tops off tomatoes. Remove pulp and stuff tomatoes with the drained mushrooms. Dot mushrooms with butter, place stuffed tomatoes in preheated 200° C (390° F) oven and bake for 10 minutes. Spoon the sauce into the artichoke bottoms on top of steaks and arrange the stuffed tomatoes around steaks on serving platter. Potato Wafers: Wash and peel potatoes, slice very thinly with a salad slicer and deep-fry till golden brown. Serve separately and sprinkle with salt.

Ingredients for 4 servings:
4 sirloin steaks, 150 g (5 oz) each
salt, pepper, 3 tablespoons oil
14 oz artichoke bottoms, canned
2 tablespoons vinegar
2 tablespoons white wine
1 green onion or 1 small onion
fresh or dried tarragon
3 egg yolks, $^1/_2$ cup butter
4 tomatoes
1 can (4 oz) button mushrooms
1 teaspoon butter
8 medium potatoes

Apricot Sherbet

Ingredients for 4 servings:
1 can apricot halves (15 oz)
$1/2$ cup sugar
2 egg whites
1 cup heavy cream
ice cold champagne

Reserve 4 of the apricot halves. Combine remaining apricot halves and their syrup with 3 tablespoons sugar and cook in a saucepan, stirring several times. Strain. Beat egg whites to a stiff meringue. Add remaining sugar to meringue and fold in carefully. Whip cream, fold it into the stiff meringue and then fold the apricot purée into this combination. Pour the resulting cream into ice trays without separators, or into a shallow dish, and freeze. To serve, cut tablespoonfuls off the frozen cream and spoon it into 4 glass serving dishes, decorating with apricot halves. Pour some champagne over each serving and serve immediately.

MENU
Mixed Salad and Ham Appetizer
Bouillon with Crepe Chips
Standing Beef Rib Roast
with Stuffed Tomatoes
Mocha Cream Dessert
(pictured on Page 105, top)

Fruity White Wine
Full-Bodied Red Wine

Mixed Salad and Ham Appetizer

Ingredients for 4 servings:
2 carrots; pinch sugar
pinch salt; $1/4$ lemon
$1/2$ salad cucumber (the long kind)
$1/2$ teaspoon prepared mustard
1 tablespoon oil
some chopped dill
$1/2$ head cauliflower
2 tablespoons cottage cheese
4 tablespoons evaporated milk;
some herbed vinegar
some pepper
pinch sugar
2 tablespoons chopped hazelnut
meats
4 to 8 slices Virginia style smoked
ham or prosciutto ham

Shred carrots and marinate with sugar, salt and lemon juice and set aside. Peel and slice cucumbers, removing the bitter tips. Combine with prepared mustard, oil and the finely chopped dill. Just before serving, season with salt to taste. Shred cauliflower finely or cut into very thin slices. Combine with cottage cheese, evaporated milk, vinegar, pepper, sugar and salt and season to taste giving the salad a lively flavor. Sprinkle with the chopped hazelnut meats and serve with the other salads; garnish salads with ham slices.

Bouillon with Crepe Chips

Ingredients for 4 servings:
4 cups broth (from cubes)
2 eggs; 2 tablespoons
evaporated milk
salt, nutmeg
1 tablespoon butter or margarine;
chopped herbs

Prepare bouillon according to instructions and heat to almost boiling. Beat together eggs and canned milk, season with salt and nutmeg and make very thin pancakes from this batter. Place pancakes on a chopping board and cut them into small squares. Add these to the hot broth and sprinkle with chopped herbs before serving.

Standing Beef Rib Roast with Stuffed Tomatoes

Ingredients for 4 servings:
1 1/2 to 2 kg (3 1/2 to 4 1/2 lb)
standing beef rib roast
salt, pepper
1 onion
1 tablespoon tomato paste
some lettuce leaves
3 teaspoons paprika
1/4 teaspoon garlic powder
some monosodium glutamate
1/2 cup butter
anchovy fillets
grated horseradish, fresh or prepared; olives; 8 tomatoes
8 medium, mealy potatoes
1 tablespoon butter or margarine;
milk
1 tablespoon grated cheese

Have butcher remove all bones from roast except rib bones; reserve bones. Tie the roast, winding a string around it 2 or 3 times. Season with salt and pepper and place in frying pan, fat side up. Roast meat in oven at 175°C (350°F) for 30 minutes per 500 g (1 lb, plus) weight. Do not turn or baste. In a skillet, brown the bones which were removed from roast, adding the cubed onion and the tomato paste. Fill up with some water or broth, cover and cook over low heat till a good sauce results. Remove rib roast from frying pan and strain sauce into pan drippings. Thicken with a little corn starch. Serve roast on platter and carve at table. Surround roast with pats of paprika butter on a bed of lettuce leaves. For paprika butter: Cream 1/2 cup butter, add 3 teaspoons paprika and a few drops lemon juice. Refrigerate till firm enough to handle, then turn out on a sheet of wax paper, roll paper around butter and shape a roll from it. Place roll in freezer for at least 1 hour, then remove wax paper and cut butter roll in slices. Also on lettuce leaves arrange anchovy fillets, horseradish and olives. Dip tomatoes in boiling water, peel and scoop out pulp. Cook and mash the potatoes, adding butter, milk and some salt and spoon the mashed potatoes into the hollow tomatoes, sprinkle with cheese and bake in preheated oven at 200°C (390°F) for 15 minutes.

Mocha Cream Dessert

Ingredients for 4 servings:
1 cup milk
2 teaspoons unflavored
gelatine
3 teaspoons instant coffee powder
1 teaspoon cocoa
1/4 teaspoon cinnamon
4 tablespoons sugar
2 cups heavy cream
1 teaspoon vanilla
1 tablespoon sugar
mocha chocolate candy or squares

Soften gelatine in 5 tablespoons cold water for 5 minutes. Bring milk to a boil. Remove from heat and stir in the powdered coffee, cocoa, cinnamon and sugar, then add the softened gelatine and stir till dissolved. Continue to stir till mixture is cool, then set aside. Whip cream and fold at least 3/4 of it into the gelatine mixture when it just begins to gel. Turn out into a dish that has been rinsed with cold water and chill. When cream is firm, unmold it onto a serving platter and garnish with the remaining whipped cream to which 1 teaspoon vanilla and 1 tablespoon sugar have been added. Decorate with mocha chocolate candy or squares. Serve fine wafers along with this dessert. Variation: Add a little rum, cherry brandy or cognac to dessert cream before it gels.

MENU

Appetizer Platter
Lady Curzon Soup
Trout in White Wine Sauce
Stuffed Veal Roast with
Potatoes Royale
Root Celery Slices
Spinach Mini-Casseroles
Fruit Salad on Lettuce
Ice Cream Bombe
(pictured on Page 105, bottom)

Light, Fruity White Wine

Appetizer Platter

Cut avocados in half lengthwise. Remove seeds and scoop out the pulp, leaving a thin lining in the half shells. Cut avocado pulp in slices and combine with the drained shrimps, chopped onion, lemon juice, salt and oil. Spoon this salad into the avocado half shells and serve on a platter along with the slices of goose breast or Canadian bacon and the asparagus spears which have been marinated with some salt, sugar and lemon juice. Peel and shred celery root, carrots and apple. Keep separate. Combine shredded celery with the chopped nut meats, some lemon juice, the cream or evaporated milk, some salt and sugar. Combine shredded carrots and apple with some lemon juice, the honey and salt, then serve on a glass serving platter, placing the celery in center and surrounding it with the carrot-apple mixture.

Ingredients for 4 servings:
2 avocados
100 g (3 ½ oz) canned shrimps
¼ onion
some lemon juice
salt, oil
100 g (3 ½ oz) smoked goose breast or Canadian bacon
1 can (14 oz) light green asparagus spears
½ celery root
3 carrots; 1 apple
1 tablespoon hazelnut meats
½ cup evaporated milk or cream; salt, sugar
1 tablespoon honey

Lady Curzon Soup

Heat turtle soup, do not boil. Take away one half of the cream and beat into it the egg yolk, salt and a little curry. Thicken turtle soup with this mixture, reheat and spoon immediately into 4 individual serving cups. Whip rest of cream and cover turtle soup with it. Dust each serving with some curry powder and place cups in hot oven till cream turns light yellow on top.

Ingredients for 4 servings:
1 can (14 oz) turtle soup
¾ cup heavy cream
1 egg yolk
salt
¾ teaspoon curry

107

Trout in White Wine Sauce

Ingredients for 4 servings:
4 trout, ready to cook
2 tablespoons butter or margarine
1 onion
1 lemon
salt, pepper
monosodium glutamate
$^1/_2$ cup white wine
1 cup milk
1 can (10$^1/_2$ oz) white sauce
1 teaspoon Worcestershire sauce
5 medium potatoes
1 tablespoon butter or margarine
2 egg yolks
some nutmeg

Remove heads from trout, wash. Grease an ovenproof platter and sprinkle it with the chopped onion. Place fish on platter. Sprinkle with lemon juice, salt, pepper, monosodium glutamate and white wine. Cover with aluminium foil and steam in oven at 175°C (350°F) for approx. 20 minutes; fish are done when they flake easily. Remove trout from oven and skin them. Add canned white sauce and Worcestershire sauce to pan juices and stir. Return fish to platter and spoon the sauce over them. Peel and quarter potatoes; boil in salted water till done. Let steam evaporate and purée the potatoes, adding butter or margarine, 1 egg yolk, salt and nutmeg. Squirt this mixture from a pastry tube on a greased baking sheet, forming rings. Brush each ring with beaten egg yolk and bake in oven for approx. 20 minutes till light golden brown on top.

Stuffed Veal Roast

Ingredients for 4 servings:
1 kg (2$^1/_4$ lb) veal rump roast
salt, pepper
4 skinless pork link
sausages
50 g (1$^3/_4$ oz) liverwurst
1 small onion
1 egg
4 tablespoons dried mushrooms
$^1/_2$ teaspoon paprika
some parsley
nutmeg, salt, pepper
250 g ($^1/_2$ lb, plus) veal bones
1 carrot; 1 onion
$^1/_4$ celery root
1 bay leaf; 2 cloves
some thyme
2 tablespoons shortening
1 tablespoon tomato paste
1$^1/_2$ cups water
2 teaspoons corn starch

Cut 1 or 2 pockets into veal roast and salt lightly inside and out. Combine pork sausage, liverwurst, chopped onion, egg and the soaked and chopped mushrooms; add paprika, chopped parsley, nutmeg, salt and pepper and work all ingredients together to make a stuffing mixture. Stuff mixture into pockets in veal and close openings with wooden skewers. In a saucepan, combine cracked veal bones, diced carrot, onion and celery root; season with bay leaf, cloves and thyme. Place meat on top of these vegetables, brush with the melted shortening and cover first with parchment paper or aluminum foil, then with lid of pan, and bake in oven for approx. 1$^1/_2$ hours at 160°C (325°F), basting 2 or 3 times. Remove meat from pan and keep warm. Add tomato paste and water to pan juices, boil up several times, then strain. Thicken pan juices with corn starch that has been dissolved in some cold water. Serve meat on platter with the side dishes described in the next three recipes.

Potatoes Royale

Ingredients for 4 servings:
10 medium potatoes
3 tablespoons oil
1 teaspoon butter
chopped parsley

Select potatoes of even size, peel and quarter. Boil potatoes up once, drain and season with salt and pepper, then bake in oven in oil till done. Sprinkle with melted butter and chopped parsley before serving.

Root Celery Slices

Ingredients for 4 servings:
1 celery root
2 tablespoons grated cheese
1 tablespoon butter

Peel celery root and cut in slices with a rippled knife. Steam in a little salted water till done. Arrange slices on an ovenproof platter or in a baking dish, sprinkle with grated cheese, dot with butter and bake briefly till just lightly browned.

Spinach Mini-Casseroles

Ingredients for 4 servings:
375 g (13 oz) frozen spinach; nutmeg
onion powder
garlic powder; 3 eggs
2 tablespoon sour cream
some paprika

Cook spinach according to package directions and blend in seasonings, eggs and salt. Spoon this mixture into greased, individual casserole dishes and place them in a shallow pan with water. Steam in oven for 30 minutes or till done. Unmold and decorate each casserole with a dollop of sour cream and dust with paprika.

Fruit Salad on Lettuce

Ingredients for 4 servings:
Lettuce leaves
1 apple (preferably red)
1 grapefruit
2 slices pineapple
some hazelnut meats
sauce Hollandaise

Peel grapefruit, remove white fibers and separate grapefruit into sections; remove membranes from individual sections. Do not peel apple, just quarter and core, then cut each quarter into thinner sections. Arrange lettuce leaves on a platter and arrange apple and grapefruit sections over them. Cut pineapple rings in quarters and distribute over the other fruit. Sprinkle with whole hazelnut meats and serve with Sauce Hollandaise (recipe on Page 143 of Appendix).

Ice Cream Bombe

Ingredients for 4 servings:
2 cups heavy cream
3 tablespoons sugar
50 g (2 oz) milk chocolate
1 teaspoon vanilla
1 tablespoon sugar
1 jigger rum or brandy
1/2 cup chopped, candied orange and lemon rind
some maraschino cherries or candied fruit
for decorating

Whip cream and blend in sugar. Break up the chocolate and dissolve in top of double boiler. Into 1/2 of the whipped cream stir the melted chocolate, vanilla, sugar and rum. Line a dome or cone shaped mold with this chocolate cream. Mix remaining half of cream with candied fruits and spoon this mixture into center of dish. Cover with wax paper or aluminum foil and freeze. Unmold and decorate with whipped cream, grated chocolate or fruits.

MENU

Fancy Venison Broth (top, insert)
Pasties with Egg and Shrimp
Ragout (top)
Stuffed Chicken Breasts and Legs
with Vegetables (bottom)
Bananas Copacabana
(pictured on Page 109)

Hearty, Distinguished
White Wine

Fancy Venison Broth

Combine ground veal with chopped pistachio nuts, sour cream and cayenne pepper. With a teaspoon, cut small dumplings from this mixture and drop in boiling, salted water. Simmer for 5 minutes; do not cook. Remove dumplings with a slotted spoon and transfer them to the broth. Season broth with sherry and serve hot.
Note: Venison broth may be substituted with beef or chicken broth.

Ingredients for 4 servings:
125 g (1/4 lb) ground veal
1 tablespoon chopped pistachio nuts
1 tablespoon sour cream
pinch cayenne pepper
2 cups venison broth (canned or fresh)
some sherry

Pasties with Egg and Shrimp Ragout

Bake patty shells according to directions. Thaw frozen shrimps in package in cold water. Boil eggs for 10 minutes, rinse with cold water, peel and cube. Wash and prepare onions, chop finely and sauté in butter or margarine till yellow. Add canned white sauce, stir and bring to a boil. Add shrimps, cubed eggs, lemon juice and dill and heat but do not boil. Season ragout to taste ans spoon into patty shells. Serve with rice and cucumber salad.

Ingredients for 4 servings:
4 patty shells
100 to 150 g (3 1/2 to 5 oz) frozen shrimps
2 eggs; 1 onion or 2 small green onions
1 tablespoon butter or margarine
1 can (10 1/2 oz) white sauce; 1/2 cup milk
juice from 1 lemon
1 tablespoon finely chopped fresh dill or 1/2 teaspoon dried dill

Stuffed Chicken Breasts and Legs with Vegetables

Quarter and bone chicken. Cut a pocket in each breast half and enlarge cuts in legs where bones have been removed to make room for stuffing. Season meat and stuff each piece with 1/2 ham slice and 1 strip of Swiss cheese. Wind a string around each piece of chicken to secure stuffing. Brown

Ingredients for 4 servings:
1 chicken
salt, pepper, thyme, marjoram
2 slices cooked ham
4 strips Swiss cheese
2 tablespoons oil

111

1 onion
1/2 cup white wine
1 pkg brown gravy mix
1 can (4 oz) sliced mushrooms

stuffed chicken pieces in oil on all sides, then cover and cook till done, approx. 30 minutes, leaving a narrow opening between lid and edge of pot to let steam escape. When meat is done, add chopped onion and sauté along with chicken till onion is light golden brown. Remove meat from pan and keep warm. Dissolve brown gravy mix according to directions and add to pan drippings. Add white wine and mushrooms and boil thoroughly. Remove strings from chicken pieces and return chicken to sauce, heating through. Serve with potatoes and with vegetables of your choice.

Bananas Copacabana

Ingredients for 4 servings:
1/2 cup water
1 small (1/2 oz) jigger rum
2 heaping tablespoons sugar
4 bananas
1 tablespoon cocoa
50 gram (2 oz) chocolate
1/2 teaspoon instant coffee powder
1 pint vanilla ice cream

Bring water, rum and sugar to a boil and set aside. Peel bananas and slice them into this sugary liquid. Return to heat and boil for 1 minute. Lift banana slices out with a slotted spoon and distribute them among 4 shallow serving dishes. Add instant coffee and chopped chocolate to sugar syrup and stir till dissolved. With a tablespoon that has been dipped in hot water, scrape curls from the ice cream and pile equal amounts of it over banana slices on serving dishes, then pour the chocolate sauce over the dessert.

MENU

Swedish Christmas Ham
(pictured on opposite page, bottom)

Christmas Punch

Swedish Christmas Ham

Ingredients for 10 servings:
approx. 3 kg (6 3/4 lb) rolled, cured ham
1 onion studded with 1 bay leaf and 2 cloves
2 carrots, halved
10 black peppercorns
1 egg white
1 teaspoon prepared mustard
1 tablespoon sugar
3 tablespoons soft, white bread crumbs without rinds

Place ham in frying pan, skin side up and fill up to 3/4 with boiling water. Add studded onion, carrots and peppercorns and cook in 160°C (325°F) oven for 2 to 3 hours or till done. Turn ham after the first 1 1/2 hours. To test for doneness, insert a long needle into ham. If needle can be pulled out easily, ham is done. Let ham cool in broth, then remove skin and most of the underlying fat, leaving just a thin layer of approx. 1 cm (3/8 inch). Beat egg whites till stiff, adding sugar and, last, the prepared mustard. Brush fat side of ham with this mixture and sprinkle with bread crumbs. Splash ham with a little melted fat, return to oven and bake approx. 50 minutes at 165°C (330°F). Serve with mashed potatoes or boiled potatoes laced with butter and sprinkled with chopped parsley.

112

For a vegetable, serve steamed red cabbage which is available commercially in jars, or prepare from basic recipe on Page 59. Add currant jelly to taste to the hot, red cabbage. Apples, steamed along with the ham or baked separately are also good accompaniments.

Christmas Punch

Ingredients for 10 servings:
6 cups red wine
1 cinnamon stick and
1 vanilla pod, each a little over
1 inch long (3 cm)
6 cloves
1 teaspoon aniseed (the last 4 ingredients will be tied in a piece of cheese cloth)
1 cup sugar
2 oranges
2 lemons
10 sugar cubes
1 cup raisins
1 cup aquavit
3 tablespoons slivered almonds

In a large, fireproof clay pan, combine red wine, seasonings and sugar and place over table burner. Rub the sugar cubes against the oranges and lemons till the thin outer skins come off and sugar cubes have absorbed the oil from the citrus peels. Plump raisins by pouring some boiling hot water over them, then place them into the aquavit along with the sugar cubes. Remove the cheese cloth with the seasonings, add aquavit, raisins and the grated rinds from oranges and lemons. Stir briefly and sprinkle slivered almonds over punch. Serve hot in punch glasses or mugs. Offer sweet or salty pastry along with this punch.

MENU

Ham Cocktail
Veal Soup "Madeira"
Turkey Drumsticks with Cranberries
Mashed Potatoes with Mixed
Vegetables; Tomato Salad
Molded Fruit Jelly
Almond Cookies
(pictured on Page 113, top)

Hearty, Distinguished
White Wine

Ham Cocktail

Ingredients for 4 servings:
125 g (4.4 oz) cooked ham
4 tomatoes
2 eggs
1 lemon
1/2 head butter lettuce
salt, pepper
vinegar
2 to 3 tablespoons oil
4 tablespoons mayonnaise
some tomato ketchup
chopped parsley

Cut ham in long strips. Peel and seed tomatoes and cut into eigths. Hard-boil eggs, peel and quarter. Cut lemon into sections. Make a marinade from the seasonings, vinegar and oil. Line stemmed serving glasses with lettuce leaves, sprinkle with some of the marinade and follow with ham strips and tomato sections. Last, pour the marinade over it all. Cut a slit on outside of each egg and lemon section and spoon some mayonnaise into it. Arrange egg and lemon sections over ham cocktail servings; garnish with tomato ketchup and parsley.

Veal Soup "Madeira"

Soak mushrooms. Heat margarine in saucepan and brown the cubed veal in it. Add the 4 chopped ingredients, dust with flour and sauté till light brown. Peel tomatoes and peppers, seed and cube. Sauté with the other vegetables. Add the soaked mushrooms with their water, pour the meat broth over it all and cook for 15 to 20 minutes. Season to taste with salt, pepper and paprika and add a dash of Madeira. Stir and serve immediately.

Ingredients for 4 servings:
2 tablespoons margarine
125 g (4 oz) cooked veal
1 tablespoon each chopped parsley, onion, celery stalks and carrots
3 tablespoons flour
2 tomatoes
2 green peppers
some dried mushrooms
4 cups meat broth
some salt and pepper
$^{1}/_{4}$ teaspoon paprika
$^{1}/_{4}$ teaspoon curry
2 tablespoons Madeira

Turkey Drumsticks with Cranberries

Season drumsticks with salt and pepper. Preheat oven to 200°C (390°F) and brown drumsticks in the hot fat on all sides; add a little water and brown meat somewhat longer, basting it with the liquid. Reduce heat to 160°C (325°F), add onion and apple, cover loosely with foil and roast for 1 to 1½ hours more. Remove drumsticks from pan, strain drippings and add enough water to make 2 cups liquid, bring to a boil and thicken with sour cream. Serve sauce separately. Surround meat on platter with orange "boats" (orange peel quarters filled with cranberries).

Ingredients for 4 servings:
4 turkey drumsticks
salt, pepper
3 to 4 tablespoons shortening or oil for frying
2 cups liquid (pan juices plus water).
1 onion
1 sour apple
$^{1}/_{2}$ cup sour cream

Mashed Potatoes with Mixed Vegetables

Wash peppers, remove seeds and pulp, then cube and boil for a minute in salted water. Heat beans in can liquid and drain. Mix with the corn kernels and sauté briefly in the hot fat, adding the finely chopped onion. Add the scalded pepper cubes and sauté along with the other vegetables. Sprinkle with chopped parsley and serve. Prepare mashed potatoes according to package directions and serve on a large platter along with the vegetables and turkey drumsticks.

Ingredients for 4 servings:
Instant mashed potatoes
for 4 servings
and required amounts of water, milk, butter, salt
2 red peppers
1 can (16 oz) each green beans and whole kernel corn
2 to 3 tablespoons margarine
1 small onion
salt, pepper, parsley

Tomato Salad

Ingredients for 4 servings:
4 to 6 tomatoes
$^1/_2$ head butter lettuce
1 onion, thinly sliced
salt, pepper, vinegar
1 to 2 tablespoons oil
chives, parsley

Cut tomatoes in thin slices. Line a serving platter with lettuce leaves, arrange tomato slices over them and top with thin onion rings. Prepare a marinade from the seasonings, vinegar and oil and spoon it over the salad. Before serving, sprinkle salad with finely chopped parsley and some chopped chives.

Molded Fruit Jelly

Ingredients for 4 servings:
2 envelopes unflavored gelatine;
3 tablespoons sugar
1 teaspoon lemon juice
1 can (14 oz) peaches
1 can (14 oz) pineapple rings
1 can (8 oz) mandarin orange sections
some maraschino cherries
1 can (14 oz) pears
4 cups fruit syrup from canned fruit
1 teaspoon unflavored gelatine
1 drop red food color
1 cup heavy cream
1 teaspoon vanilla
1 tablespoon sugar

Soften gelatine in 5 tablespoons cold water for 5 minutes. Mix the syrup from the canned fruits and measure off 4 cups. Pour $^1/_2$ cup of the syrup into a small saucepan and heat just to boiling. Dissolve the softened gelatine in the hot syrup, stirring constantly. Stir the sugar and the lemon juice into the remaining $3^1/_2$ cups fruit syrup, then add the hot fruit syrup with the dissolved gelatine.
Pour a small amount of the syrup mixture into a shallow mold or dish; refrigerate till it gels. Arrange some of the mixed fruits on top of this layer. Follow with some more syrup, allow to gel and top with another layer of fruit. Add a drop (or more, if required) red food color to the remaining sirup mixture and pour it over the last layer of fruits. Refrigerate till the next day, then unmold on a platter and garnish with the whipped cream that has been sweetened with 1 tablespoon sugar and flavored with 1 teaspoon vanilla.

Almond Cookies

Ingredients for 4 servings:
150 g (5 oz) blanched, grated almonds
$1^1/_3$ cup powdered sugar
2 level tablespoons flour
4 tablespoons butter or margarine
6 egg whites
100 g (3.5 oz) milk chocolate

Combine grated almonds, sugar and flour. Beat egg whites to a stiff meringue. Melt the fat and fold both the meringue and the almond mixture into it, making a soft, creamy paste. With a teaspoon, cut walnut-size mounds off this paste and place them on a greased cookie sheet, flattening each mound somewhat with the back of a spoon. Bake cookies approx. 5 minutes in 200°C (390°F) oven till their edges are golden yellow. Melt milk chocolate in top of double boiler and sandwich two cookies together at a time after brushing their facing sides with some of the chocolate. Place on rack to dry.

Quail Eggs with Cress Butter
(bottom) and Remoulade
Tarragon Chicken Broth (top, left)
Shrimp au Gratin (top, right)
Saddle of Venison, Fancy
with Stuffed Pears
Brussels Sprouts, Potato Croquettes
Caramel Cream
(partially pictured on Page 117)

_____

Celebrated White Wine
Full-Bodied Red Wine

Quail Eggs with Cress Butter and Remoulade

Ingredients for 4 servings:
32 quail eggs
salt water
125 g (1/4 lb) watercress
4 tablespoons butter
salt, pepper
2 sour pickles
1/4 onion
1 teaspoon capers
some chopped parsley
1/2 cup mayonnaise

Place quail eggs in cold, salted water, bring to a boil and boil for 2 minutes. Drain and immediately rinse with cold water. Peel one half of the quail eggs immediately and arrange them on a large platter on a bed of watercress; surround with the unpeeled eggs to display their speckled beauty. For a colorful effect, cut some of the peeled eggs in half. Serve with cress butter which is prepared as follows: Stir butter with salt and pepper and add 1 tablespoon chopped cress, mixing well. Remoulade dressing also goes well with these eggs; you prepare it from pickles, onion, capers and parsley, all chopped together and stirred into the mayonnaise. Serve with slices from long loaves of French bread. Note: You can order quail eggs through delicatessen and gourmet dealers.

Tarragon Chicken Broth

Ingredients for 4 servings:
3 cups chicken broth (cubes)
some white wine
3 tablespoons fresh
(or 1 1/4 teaspoons dried)
tarragon

Prepare 3 cups chicken broth from cubes or use fresh broth. Chop fresh tarragon coarsely and simmer 2 tablespoons of it in the broth for 5 minutes (or use dried tarragon instead). Add white wine to taste and strain broth. If fresh tarragon is available, sprinkle 1 tablespoon fresh chopped tarragon leaves over broth before serving.

Shrimp au Gratin

Thaw shrimps in cold water in package. Wash and prepare mushrooms and cut in thick slices. Chop onion and sauté in the hot margarine for 3 minutes. Add the sliced mushrooms, season with pepper and sauté for 5 minutes more. Add white wine and bring to a boil. Beat together sour cream and flour, add to skillet, stir and boil thoroughly. Stir in the shrimps and do not cook any more. Season to taste. Stir together grated cheese and egg yolks. If desired, add 2 tablespoons white wine or sour cream. Spoon the hot shrimp mixture into 4 large half shells or fireproof ragout fin dishes and brush with cheese mixture. Place under broiler till crust is light golden yellow.

Ingredients for 4 servings:
150 g (5 oz) frozen shrimps
250 g (1/2 lb, plus) fresh mushroom
1 onion or 4 green onions
1 teaspoon margarine
some ground, white pepper
1/2 cup white wine
1/2 cup sour cream
2 level teaspoons flour
some cayenne pepper and tarragon
juice from 1/4 lemon
Worcestershire sauce
some salt
1/2 cup grated cheese
2 egg yolks

Saddle of Venison, Fancy

Remove membrane from saddle of vension and lard the meat with thin strips of fat bacon; season with salt and pepper. Heat fat in frying pan, place saddle of vension in it, back down, and brown it quickly. Turn meat and add the cubed onions and carrots. Place in oven and roast at 225°C (440°F) for 40 minutes, basting several times with the drippings. When done, pour cream and meat broth over it. Lift meat out of pan, remove bone, and cut loin strips diagonally into thick slices. Strain sauce and serve separately in sauce boat. Serve meat on a hot platter, surrounded with pear halves filled with currant jelly. Side dish: Mushrooms (preferably chanterelles), Brussels sprouts, potato croquettes (recipe on Page 59).

Ingredients for 4 servings:
Approx. 1 kg (2 1/4 lb) saddle of vension
2 strips smoked bacon (fat)
salt, pepper
2 tablespoons butter or margarine
1 onion
1 carrot
1 cup heavy cream
1/2 cup meat broth (cubes)
6 canned pear halves
some currant jelly

Caramel Cream

Ingredients for 4 servings:
1 tablespoon butter or margarine
$1/2$ cup sugar
$1/2$ cup water
2 cups milk
6 eggs
2 teaspoons vanilla
5 tablespoons sugar

Melt butter or margarine, add sugar and caramelize, stirring constantly. Add water and stir, cooking all ingredients into a thick syrup. Pour this syrup into four metal molds or coffee cups, set aside till hard and crusty. Bring milk to a boil, beat together the sugar, beaten eggs, and the vanilla. Pour this milk and egg mixture over the caramel in the molds or cups and place them in a shallow pan filled with hot water. Cover pan, leaving a narrow opening. Keep water in pan hot over very low heat, do not boil. Cream will be done after 40 minutes. Refrigerate caramel cream, then unmold onto serving plates. Dissolve the residue at the bottom of each mold with some hot water and pour some of this sauce around each serving.

MENU

*Scrambled Eggs and Anchovies
on Toast (top, right)
Broiled or Grilled Tartar
Beef Steaks with Vegetable Purée (bottom)
Orange Cream with Bananas
(top, left)
(pictured on Page 120)*

Sparkling White Wine

Scrambled Eggs with Anchovies on Toast

Ingredients for 4 servings:
4 eggs
2 tablespoons white wine
ground, white pepper
4 slices sandwich bread
1 teaspoon margarine
1 can anchovy fillets (2 oz) chives
lemon slices

Beat together eggs and white wine and some ground white pepper. Toast bread slices. Melt margarine, scramble egg mixture in hot fat in skillet. Distribute scrambled eggs over the 4 toast slices and top each portion with 2 anchovy fillets. Sprinkle with the chopped chives and serve with thin lemon slices that may be garnished with sprigs of dill.

Broiled Tartar Beef Steaks

Combine ground sirloin, salt, pepper, nutmeg and egg and shape into 4 patties. Oil and heat a broiling skillet and broil tartar steaks in it 4 minutes on each side which will leave them slightly rare on inside. Top Tartar steaks with a few thin onion slices and spoon some prepared horseradish into center of each onion ring. For the mixed vegetables, wash and peel celery roots, potatoes and carrots and cut them in large cubes approx. 1 inch (2 ½ cm). Sauté the sliced onions in margarine till light yellow, then add the cubed vegetables. Pour 1 cup water over them, season with salt and pepper, cover and steam till done. When all vegetables are done, purée them in blender or force through a sieve. Season to taste with nutmeg. Serve on platter with tomato sections and parsley.

Ingredients for 4 servings:
400 g (14 oz) leanest ground sirloin
salt, pepper
1 egg
nutmeg
2 tablespoons oil
3 onions
1 tablespoon grated horseradish, fresh or prepared
1 tablespoon margarine
500 g (1 lb, plus) carrots
400 g (14 oz) root celery
3 medium potatoes

Orange Cream with Bananas

Separate eggs and beat together egg yolks, sugar and vanilla till mixture is light and fluffy. Soften gelatine in 5 tablespoons cold water for 5 minutes. In a small saucepan, combine lemon and orange juice and heat just to boiling. Add the softened gelatine and stir till dissolved. Beat in egg yolk mixture and refrigerate the resulting cream till it begins to set. In the meantime, peel and mash bananas with fork, whip cream. Beat the 2 egg whites till they stand up in soft peaks. Fold mashed bananas, whipped cream and beaten egg whites into orange cream which is just beginning to set. Spoon cream into stemmed serving glasses, alternating with orange sections, and refrigerate till firm.

Ingredients for 4 servings:
2 eggs, separated
2 ¼ tablespoons sugar
1 teaspoon vanilla
1 teaspoon unflavored gelatine
juice from ½ lemon
½ cup freshly squeezed orange juice
2 or 3 ripe bananas
½ cup heavy cream
1 jigger rum or brandy
2 oranges, peeled and separated in sections

MENU

Cheese Mini-Sandwiches and
Cheese Puffs (top, right)
Stuffed Suckling Pig with
Kraut Salad and Variety
Potata Salad (bottom)
Ice Cream Stuffed Apples (top, left)
(pictured on Page 121)

Cheese Mini-Sandwiches

(8 servings)
Alternate 8 buttered slices of square pumpernickel with 7 slices sharp cheddar cheese; wrap in wax paper and place in refrigerator for some time, weighing the package down to make slices stick together. Unwrap, cut in cubes and garnish with olives, grapes or anything suitable.

Cheese Puffs

(8 servings)
Ingredients: 1 cup water, salt
$^1/_2$ cup plus 1 tablespoon butter or margarine
1$^1/_2$ cups flour
4 eggs
2 egg yolks
butter
camembert cheese
chopped nuts

Prepare an eclair dough (recipe on Page 144 of Appendix) from the water, salt, butter, flour and eggs plus egg yolks and squirt onto a well-greased baking sheet in mounds the size of walnuts. Bake approx. 15 minutes at 200°C (390°F). Filling: Cream together 1 part butter and 1 part camembert cheese. Cut puffs open, fill with the cheese cream, sprinkle filling with chopped nuts and replace tops which may be garnished if desired.

124

Table Setting for a First Communion or Confirmation Dinner

Table Setting for an Easter Dinner

Stuffed Suckling Pig

Ingredients for 8 servings:
1 suckling pig (approx.
5 kg or 11 lb), ready to cook, plus
the liver
salt, pepper
5 green onions
2 jiggers brandy
6 strips smoked bacon
1 onion
5 pork link sausages, skinless
3 stale rolls
2 eggs
salt, pepper, thyme, parsley
2 cups oil
2 cups dark beer

Meat must be aged 1 day. Rub suckling pig with salt and pepper inside and out. Season on inside with chopped green onions and brandy. Sauté the diced bacon and chopped onion till light yellow, then add cubed liver and quickly brown on all sides, stirring constantly. Add pork sausage and soaked, stale rolls, eggs, salt, pepper, thyme and chopped parsley and mix well. Stuff this mixture into suckling pig and sew up. Turn legs under till they snap and place suckling pig in a frying pan. Wrap ears and tail in aluminum foil to prevent burning. Roast suckling pig in oven for approx. 2 1/2 to 3 hours at 160°C (325°F), brushing it with oil from time to time and basting with dark beer. At end of roasting time, suckling pig should be brown and crisp and stuffing well done. Carve with poultry carving shears or electric knife.

Kraut Salad

Ingredients for 8 servings:
1 small head cabbage
salt, vinegar, pepper
1 onion, chopped
1 clove garlic
chopped herbs
4 strips smoked bacon

Cut cabbage in fine strips, season with salt, pepper and vinegar and place in a large, shallow container; weigh down with a water-filled dish for 2 to 3 hours. Then combine cabbage, chopped onion, garlic, herbs and the bacon which has been cut in thin strips and crisped. Mix the crisp bacon and its drippings into the cabbage salad; toss and serve lukewarm.

Variety Potato Salad

Boil potatoes in their jackets, peel and slice while still warm. Marinate potato slices with salt, pepper, vinegar and oil. Peel and cut tomatoes, remove seeds, cube tomatoes and add them to the salad. Add the chopped pickles and olives. Set aside to marinate, then serve salad attractively on platter, sprinkling the cocktail onions over it. Decorate with fans that are cut from cucumbers (see illustration).

Ingredients for 8 servings:
8 medium potatoes
salt, pepper, vinegar, oil
2 tomatoes
2 sour pickles
5 green olives
For decorating:
Some cocktail onions,
tomatoes and cucumbers

Ice Cream Stuffed Apples

Peel apples and leave stems on. Cut off bottom parts (with the stems); core apples. Bring water, white wine, lemon juice and sugar to a boil; simmer apples and their „lids" in this syrup for 5 minutes. Do not boil. Then set aside to cool in the syrup. Lift apples out and drain well. Place on glass serving dishes and refrigerate. Mix the syrup with the jam or jelly and add some rum, blackberry liqueur or orange liqueur. Scoop the ice cream into the apples, cover with „lids" and pour the red syrup around them and serve immediately.

Ingredients for 8 servings:
8 medium apples (Golden Delicious)
1 cup water
2 cups white wine
juice from 1 lemon
4 tablespoons sugar
3 tablespoons red jam or jelly
8 scoops Neapolitan ice cream

MENU

Italian Boiled Meat with Green Sauce

Ingredients for 8 servings:
Approx. 4 liters (quarts) water
salt
1 fresh beef tongue (approx. 1 kg
or 2 1/4 lb)
1 stewing chicken, ready to cook
(approx. 1 1/2 kg or 3 1/2 lb)
1 kg (2 1/4 lb) beef short ribs
1 kg (2 1/4 lb) rolled veal shoulder
250 g (1/2 lb, plus) Polish style sausage with garlic
3 onions
4 carrots
some parsley
2 bay leaves
some green celery tops
1 teaspoon thyme
4 cloves garlic
1 teaspoon white peppercorns
For the soup:
250 g (1/2 lb, plus) egg noodles,
8 cups broth from the meat
For the sauce:
2 onions
2 cloves garlic
2 tablespoons chopped parsley
1/2 teaspoon basil
4 sour pickles
1 tablespoon capers
1/2 teaspoon thyme
1/2 cup wine vinegar
1 cup olive oil
salt, pepper

In a large kettle, bring water and salt to a boil, add beef tongue and stewing chicken and boil for 1 1/2 hours. Add beef short ribs and continue to boil. Peel and halve the onion. Wash and scrape the carrots. Crush the unpeeled garlic cloves. Tie celery greens, bay leaves and parsley in a piece of cheese cloth. After another half hour, add all these ingredients to kettle, plus the white peppercorns and the veal shoulder and boil for one more hour. Lift meat out of broth and keep warm. Skin tongue. Heat garlic sausage in the broth. Strain broth, cook noodles in it and serve as soup.
For the sauce: Peel onions and garlic and chop finely. Also, chop parsley and pickles and the capers; add thyme. Combine all these ingredients, stir in vinegar and oil and season to taste with salt and pepper.

Table Settings for a Wedding Dinner

Crepes "Artemis"

Ingredients for 8 servings:
1¹/₃ cups flour
2 teaspoons vanilla
2 tablespoons sugar
2 pinches salt
2 cups milk
6 eggs
1 cup plus 4 tablespoons butter
300 g (10¹/₂ oz) nougat
2 pints vanilla ice cream
2 tablespoons sugar
juice from 4 oranges
some grated orange rind
1 cup flaming cherry brandy (or flaming brandy)

Combine flour, sugar and salt in a bowl. Add milk, 4 whole eggs and 2 egg yolks, and stir in the vanilla, making a thin batter. Melt ¹/₃ of the butter and beat into the batter. In a non-stick skillet, bake 16 thin pancakes without using any fat. Let pancakes cool. Melt nougat in top of double boiler and spread over pancakes, leaving a 2 cm (approx. 1 inch) edge around each pancake. Cut ice cream into 16 equal portions and place 1 portion in center of each crepe. Brush edges of crepes with egg whites, roll up and place in freezer for approx. 10 minutes. In a shallow saucepan, melt remaining butter and sugar till light yellow. Add orange juice and grated orange rind and cook, stirring constantly, till liquid is partially evaporated. Place pancakes into thickened sauce and pour the flaming cherry brandy (or brandy) over them, ignite, burn off and serve immediately.

MENU

Watercress or Dandelion Salad
Legs of Hare "St. Hubert"
with Nut Potato Balls and Vegetables
Orange Fritters with Vanilla Sauce
(not pictured)
___
Celebrated, Elegant Red Wine

Watercress or Dandelion Salad

Ingredients for 4 servings:
200 g (7 oz) watercress or young dandelion leaves
1 onion
4 tablespoons mayonnaise
juice from 1 lemon
pepper
1 teaspoon prepared mustard
salt
2 tablespoons chopped walnuts

Wash and prepare leaves. Cut onion into rings and mix with the leaves. Combine mayonnaise, sour cream, lemon juice, pepper, mustard and salt. Spoon this sauce over salad and sprinkle with chopped walnuts.

Legs of Hare "St. Hubert" with Nut Potato Balls and Vegetables

Remove membranes from legs of hare. Season with salt and pepper and wrap $^1/_2$ bacon slice around each leg; fasten in place with string. Quickly brown meat on all sides in hot oil. Add chopped onion, bay leaf and juniper berries and roast meat in oven at 190°C (375°F) for 1 hour. Add the red wine to pan juices before thickening the sauce. Beat together cream and flour, stir into pan liquid and boil up, then strain. Heat the puréed chestnuts. Peel, halve and core apples; sprinkle with sugar and place under broiler till done. Top each half with some of the hot chestnut purée. For the nut potato balls: Peel, cook and mash potatoes; combine with 2 egg yolks, some salt and nutmeg. Shape walnut size balls from mixture. Dip potato balls first in egg white, then roll in the coarsely chopped hazelnut meats. Fry in deep fat at 180° C (360° F) till done. Remove strings from legs of hare and serve meat on platter with the apple halves; arrange some grapes around it all. Serve potato balls and sauce separately. Side dishes are Brussels sprouts or steamed red cabbage (recipe for red cabbage on Page 59), or use steamed red cabbage from jars.

Ingredients for 4 servings:
2 legs of hare
salt, pepper
2 slices bacon
2 tablespoons oil
1 onion
1 bay leaf
5 juniper berries
$^1/_2$ cup red wine
$^1/_2$ cup heavy cream
1 teaspoon flour
1 cup puréed chestnuts (from can)
2 apples
1 teaspoon sugar
some grapes
5 medium potatoes
some nutmeg
2 eggs
3 tablespoons coarsely chopped hazelnuts

1. Place Setting for:
Soup
Meat main course
Cold dessert
Beverages: White wine
Red wine

2. Place Setting for:
Soup
Warm Appetizer
Fish main course
Meat main course
Cold dessert
Beverages: White wine
Red wine
Champagne

3. Place Setting for:
Soup
Meat main course
Fish main course
Warm dessert
Beverages: White wine
Champagne

Table Setting for an Engagement Dinner

Table Setting for an Anniversary Dinner

Orange Fritters with Vanilla Sauce

Ingredients for 4 servings:
4 oranges
1 tablespoon powdered sugar
1 jigger Grand Marnier or rum
For the batter:
1/2 cup beer
1 teaspoon sugar
1 egg
pinch salt
4 1/2 tablespoons flour
Vanilla Sauce:
2 cups milk
1 vanilla pod
2 egg yolks
2 tablespoon sugar
1 tablespoon corn starch

Peel oranges, remove white fibers and cut oranges in slices of approx. 1 cm (³/8 inch). Marinate orange slices with powdered sugar and Grand Marnier or rum. To make batter, beat together beer, sugar, eggs, salt and flour. Dip marinated orange slices in batter and fry in deep fat at 180°C (360°F) till golden yellow.

Vanilla Sauce: Cut vanilla pod open, place in milk in saucepan and bring to a boil; remove from heat. Beat together egg yolk, sugar and corn starch and add this mixture to the milk, return to heat and boil up once more. Serve orange fritters with vanilla sauce poured over them, or serve sauce separately in a pitcher.

MENU

Toast with Ham and Melted Cheese
Lamb Chops Provençale
with Green Beans and Whole, Fried Potatoes
Fruit Cocktail with Almonds
(not pictured)

Tasty White Wine or Rosé

Toast with Ham and Melted Cheese

Ingredients for 4 servings:
4 slices white sandwich bread
4 slices cooked ham
1 teaspoon prepared mustard
4 slices Tilsit cheese
cayenne pepper

Toast bread slices and top with the ham slices. Brush ham with mustard and top with cheese. Place toast slices under broiler just until cheese melts. Dust lightly with cayenne pepper and serve very hot.

Lamb Chops "Provençale" with Green Beans and Whole, Fried Potatoes

Cut or buy the meat in 4 large or 8 small chops; season with salt and pepper. Heat oil and fry chops in it till done, but do not overcook. Add butter or margarine to drippings and sauté the finely diced onions in it till golden yellow; mix in the crushed garlic, parsley and the thyme. Simmer chops briefly in this seasoning mix; serve with green beans and whole, small fried potatoes.

Ingredients for 4 servings:
750 g (1 ½ lb, plus) lamb chops
salt, pepper
1 tablespoon oil
1 teaspoon butter or margarine
2 onions
2 cloves garlic
1 tablespoon chopped parsley
¼ teaspoon thyme

Fruit Cocktail with Almonds

Combine fruit sirup from can with sugar, bring to a boil and boil for approx. 5 minutes. Add vanilla. Slice bananas and add to fruit sirup; set aside to cool. Add the drained fruits and the prepared berries. Also, add lemon juice and brandy or one of the other choices and refrigerate for approx. 1 hour. Sprinkle with grated nuts or toasted, slivered almonds. Serve with whipped cream if desired.

Ingredients for 4 servings:
1 can (12 oz) fruit cocktail
1 teaspoon vanilla
3 ½ tablespoons sugar
2 bananas
250 g (½ lb, plus) berries (strawberries, raspberries, blackberries, or currants) juice from 1 lemon
2 jiggers brandy, Grand Marnier, cherry brandy or maraschino
almond slivers or grated nutmeats

MENU

Cold Trout with Herbed Sauce

Ingredients for 4 servings:
4 trout, 200 g (7 oz) each, ready
to cook
salt, vinegar
6 tomatoes
1 can (4 oz) sliced mushrooms
4 olives
2 carrots
$^1/_2$ celery root
pepper
1 lemon
$^1/_2$ cup mayonnaise
parsley, dill, chives
Worcestershire sauce

Bend each trout into a ring, tying head and tail together, and place in hot water to which some salt and vinegar have been added. Simmer for 10 minutes, then set aside to cool. Remove skin from back of each fish and garnish backs with 2 of the tomatoes which have been peeled and quartered, and with the sliced mushrooms and sliced olives. Cut carrots and celery in strips and cook in a little salted water till done. Season with salt, pepper and lemon juice and set aside. Peel the remaining 4 tomatoes, cut off tops and scoop out pulp. Stuff tomatoes with the vegetable salad. Serve trout on platter and surround with the stuffed tomatoes. Prepare an herb sauce from the mayonnaise and the chopped herbs, season with Worcestershire sauce, lemon juice and salt and serve sauce along with fish.

Young Guinea Hen, Vintager Style

Ingredients for 4 servings:
2 guinea hens, ready to cook
(pheasants may be substituted)
salt, pepper, juniper berries
2 large, thin slices of fat bacon
3 tablespoons oil
1 onion
1 carrot
$^1/_2$ tablespoon tomato paste
1 tablespoon flour
1 $^1/_2$ cups meat broth (cubes)
$^1/_2$ bay leaf
1 cup sour cream
some lemon juice

Season guinea hens with salt, pepper and crushed juniper berries. Place bacon slices on breasts and tie in place with thread. Roast guinea hens in oven at 190°C (375°F) for 40 minutes or till done. After the first 20 minutes, add the diced onion and carrot. After 30 minutes, remove bacon slices from breasts of guinea hens so they'll become crisp and brown. Dice bacon slices and crisp them in skillet. Split guinea hens in half lengthwise and sprinkle the crisp bacon around them. Stir tomato paste into pan drippings and brown, then add broth and bay leaf and cook for 10 minutes. Stir in the sour cream and strain sauce. Season with salt and pepper, add a little lemon juice and serve separately in sauce boat.

136

Wine Kraut

Turn sauerkraut out in colander and rinse quickly to remove excess acid. Cut onion and apples in slices and sauté in the hot fat in saucepan till yellow. Add sauerkraut, wine, water, bay leaf and clove. Cover and cook approx. 1 hour over low heat. Finally, stir in the grapes and season with salt.

Ingredients for 4 servings:
1 (20 oz) can sauerkraut
1 tablespoon butter or margarine
1 onion
2 apples
1 cup white wine
1 cup water
$1/2$ bay leaf
1 clove
1 cup light grapes
salt

Pineapple Cocktail with Vanilla Ice Cream

Cut the top off a fresh pineapple and scoop out the fruit pulp, taking care not to damage the shell. Remove hard inner core from fruit pulp, cube pineapple pulp, marinate to taste with Cointreau and sugar and chill. Serve the fruit in the pineapple shell on crushed ice. Serve vanilla ice cream individually and have guests help themselves to pineapple cocktail from the pineapple half shells.

Appendix

Potato Dumplings

Ingredients for 4 servings:
4 medium potatoes
1 egg
$^1/_2$ cup flour
2 tablespoons corn starch
$^1/_4$ teaspoon salt
$^1/_8$ teaspoon paprika
2 shakes white ground pepper
2 shakes onion salt
2 slices stale bread
1 tablespoon butter or margarine

Peel potatoes and cook in salted water till done; drain and shake pot briefly over heat sorce to dry potatoes out, then set aside to cool off and later refrigerate for 2 to 3 hours. Soak 1 of the bread slices in water. Grate the chilled potatoes and add the well beaten egg, the flour, corn starch and seasonings and knead all ingredients into a smooth dough, adding the soaked bread slice from which the water has been squeezed. Refrigerate dough briefly. In the meantime, melt the butter or margarine in a skillet, cube the second bread slice and sauté in the hot fat till golden brown on both sides. Shape 8 balls from the dough, dipping hands in water before rolling each dumpling, then push one or two of the crisp bread cubes into the center of each dumpling. Drop dumplings into rapidly boiling, slightly salted water; do not cover. Dumplings are done when they float to the surface. Remove with slotted spoon and serve the well drained dumplings separately or arrange on same platter with main dish.

Curry Sauce

Ingredients for 4 servings:
2 tablespoons butter or margarine
1 onion
2 tablespoons flour
1 cup scalded milk
$^3/_4$ cup meat broth
some thyme, mutmeg
and ground white pepper
1$^1/_2$ teaspoons curry powder
grated rind from $^1/_2$ lemon
$^1/_2$ teaspoon ground turmeric
2 tablespoons brandy (optional)

Peel and dice onions and sauté in the butter or margarine till light yellow. Add the flour and heat till yellow, stirring constantly. Add milk, meat broth, thyme, nutmeg, white pepper, turmeric, brandy, lemon rind and curry powder; beat with wire whisk, cover and simmer over low heat for 10 minutes. Serve immediately with main dish.

Lobster Butter

Cream $^1/_4$ cup butter with 2 tablespoons cooked lobster meat, ground or mashed; stir in $^1/_2$ teaspoon fresh lemon juice.

Steamed Kohlrabi

Try this tender and economic summer vegetable

Remove and discard the coarse outer leaves. Reserve the tender inner leaves and cut in strips. Peel the kohlrabi carefully, starting at root and pulling upward which makes the peel very thin toward the top. Cut the peeled kohlrabi first in half, then in thin wedges. Dice onion and sautée in the butter or margarine. Add kohlrabi, water, salt and sugar, cover and simmer for 20 minutes. After 15 minutes, add the young leaves. If desired, stir in 1/2 cup heavy cream, heat through and serve. This vegetable goes well with ham or meat loaf.

Ingredients for 4 servings:
6–8 kohlrabi
1 onion
2 tablespoons butter or margarine
1 cup water
1 pinch salt
1 pinch suger
Calories: Approx. 120 per serving

Clear Oxtail Soup (Basic Recipe)

Briefly fry the oxtail sections in the hot margarine on all sides but do not let them turn brown. Add the prepared vegetables and fry all these ingredients together, stirring several times. After about 10 minutes, add the tomato paste and season to taste with the listed seasonings except monosodium glutamate, salt and sherry. Add the water and some salt, bring to a boil and turn heat down. Remove lid from kettle and simmer the soup very slowly till meat is done. Immediately pour entire contents of kettle through a strainer, remove meat from bones, cube and return to the clear broth. Season to taste with monosodium glutamate, some more salt and a dash sherry. Serve piping hot.

Ingredients:
Approx. 1 kg (2 1/4 lb) oxtail sections
6 tablespoons margarine
2 carrots, diced
1 leek, diced
1/4 celery root, diced
1 onion, diced
5 cups water
1 tablespoon tomato paste
1 bay leaf
some thyme
   coriander
   ground black pepper
   ground clove
   garlic powder
   monosodium glutamate
   salt
dash sherry

Pickled Pumpkins

Ingredients for 10 servings:
2 kg (4.4 lb) pumpkin
cleaned, peeled and cubed
5 cups white vinegar
5 cups water
1 to 2 cups wine vinegar
1 kg (2.2 lb) sugar
1 lemon
1 stick ginger

Place the cubed pumpkins in an ironstone or earthenware dish or crock. Combine white vinegar and water and pour over pumpkin cubes; marinate till the next day. Turn pumpkin cubes out in a colander to drain. In a saucepan, combine wine vinegar, sugar, ginger, the grated rind and the juice from the lemon and bring these ingredients to a boil. Add the drained pumpkin cubes and cook over low heat till they begin to look glassy. Lift pumpkin cubes out of liquid with a slotted spoon and transfer them to an earthenware dish or crock. Continue to cook liquid till it thickens; then remove from heat and pour over the pumpkin cubes. Let cool. Cover with cellophane and tie it securely over dish. Refrigerate. This makes a delicious condiment or dessert.

Paté Seasoning

To make 1 batch, mix the following ingredients and keep in a jar:

1 tablespoon each of the following **ground** spices:

Cloves; ginger; white pepper; black pepper; bay leaf (crushed); nutmeg; mace; basil (crushed); thyme and 1/2 tablespoon marjoram

Vanilla Cream

Ingredients for 4 Servings:
1 cup milk
4 egg yolks
2 egg whites
4 tablespoons sugar
1 teaspoon vanilla
1 envelope unflavored gelantine
1 cup whipping cream

Soften gelatine in 5 tablespoons cold water. Bring milk to a boil. Stir together egg yolks, sugar and vanilla, add the milk and beat these combined ingredients in top of double boiler over hot water till a thick, frothy cream results. Into this hot cream, stir the softened gelantine and continue to stir till mixture is cool and gelantine is completely dissolved. Refrigerate briefly. Beat the egg whites till stiff, whip the cream, and fold these two ingredients into the refrigerated gelantine mixture just before it sets. Pour into serving dishes and refrigerate for several hours; unmold and serve.

Ragout Fin (Basic recipe)

Bring to a boil the meat, 1 1/2 cups water, onion studded with 1 clove and 1 bay leaf, the celery leaves, a dash of salt and the juice from 1/2 lemon. Cover and cook over low heat till meat is tender. Lift meat out of broth, let cool somewhat and cut in small cubes. Combine the remaining lemon juice with cream, Worcesterhire sauce, egg yolk and corn starch and stir well. Reheat 1 cup of the meat broth to the boiling point and stir this mixture into the broth, boiling up just once, then turn off heat. Season the sauce to taste with salt and monosodium glutamate. Should sauce be too thick, thin it down with some more broth. Return cubes meat to the sauce and heat through but do not boil.

Ingredients:
250 gram (1/2 lb, plus) boneless veal
1 onion, 1 clove, 1 bay leaf
a few celery leaves
salt
juice from 1 lemon
1/2 cup heavy cream
1/2 teaspoon Worcesterhire sauce
1 egg yolk
1 heaping tablespoon corn starch
dash monosodium glutamate
1 1/2 cups water

Sauce Hollandais

This is a popular accompaniment for asparagus or cauliflower

In double boiler, beat egg yolks, lukewarm water and lemon juice till thick and creamy. Remove top of double boiler from water base. Melt butter and margarine together and add to creamy mixture by the drop, stirring constantly; this sauce must not be overheated or it may curdle. To keep sauce warm, return it to base of double boiler but do not reheat water in boiler.

Ingredients for 8 servings:
3 egg yolks
1/2 cup lukewarm water
1 teaspoon lemon juice
125 gram (approx 1/4 lb) butter
125 gram (approx. 1/4 lb) margarine
salt
pinch white, ground pepper

Cream Puffs (Basic)

Ingredients for 8 servings:
1 cup water
salt
$^1/_2$ cup plus 1 tablespoon butter
4 eggs
2 egg yolks

Bring water, butter and salt to a boil. Sift the flour and add the whole amount at once to the water, stirring constantly until the resulting paste no longer sticks to bottom and sides of pan and begins to take the shape of a ball. Place dough in a deep dish and immediately stir in 1 egg. Wait 10 minutes, then work in the remaining eggs, one by one. Grease a baking sheet and dust with flour. Place small mounds of the dough on sheet, approx. 1$^1/_2$ inches apart, and brush with the beaten egg yolks. Bake in oven at 225° C (440° F) for 30 minutes. Do not open oven while pastry is baking. At end of baking time, turn off heat and leave pastry in oven for another 10 minutes to dry. Remove from oven, cut each puff in half, let cool and fill with a savory filling.

Some "Household Metrics"

The metric system is simple. It is based on the number 10. The name "metric" comes from the principal unit of length in this system, which is the meter. One meter has 100 centimeters, one centimeter has 10 millimeters. It's exactly the same as with dollars and cents: One dollar has 100 cents, one dime has 10 cents – this means you are already familiar with the metric system.

How long is a meter? One meter is just a little more than one yard. Strictly speaking, one yard equals 0.9144 meter. One inch is about 2½ centimeters. Strictly speaking, one inch equals 2.54 centimeters. The abbreviation for meter is m, for centimeter cm. A nine-inch pie pan, in metric language, would be 23-cm pie pan. Strictly speaking, it would be 2 millimeters (mm) short of 23 cm; but in the kitchen, who needs to speak all that strictly? After all, we are talking about pie pans, not scientific instruments. To show you the conversion at a glance, here is a ruler with both inches and centimeters:

INCHES VS. CENTIMETERS

When it comes to liquid measure, the basic metric unit is the liter. One liter equals about 1 quart. The difference is minimal, for one US liquid quart equals 0.946 liter. So, for household purposes, you just tell yourself that one liter is one quart – a teaspoon more or less will not blow up the laboratory (or should we say the kitchen?). For smaller quantities, you can go right on calling them by the familiar names, for 1 pint is almost exactly ½ liter, and 1 cup is ¼ liter. You see, metrics really need not cause an uproar in the kitchen.

Now, what about weight? You are used to thinking in ounces and pounds. Already, as you study the can labels in the supermarkets, you find the contents given in both ounces and grams. One ounce has 28.4 grams. Sixteen ounces, or one US pound, equals 454 grams. Compared to ½ kilo (which might be called a metric pound), it falls short by 46 grams because ½ kilo equals 500 grams, and 1 kilo, of course, is 1 000 grams. Incidentally, when you step on a metric scale, you'll be delighted to see that you tip at a much lower figure (but you still weigh the same!).

What does all this mean for your cooking and baking? The Burda cook books speak your language. We know that you are used to measuring, not weighing, your ingredients; so we have adapted the quantities to cups, tablespoons and teaspoons – you just go on doing what you used to while, actually, you **are** tuning in to the metric system.

How about cooking and baking temperatures? Thermometers and appliances of the future will show the temperatures in centigrade instead of Fahrenheit; here again, the prefix "centi" stands for 100. Just as 100 cents make one dollar, 100 grades (or divisions) make up the scale of the centigrade thermometer between freezing and boiling point. Water freezes at 0 °C and boils at 100 °C (at sea level, that is). How do you convert given temperatures from centigrade to Fahrenheit or vice versa? You divide the centigrade value by 5, then multiply it with 9 and add 32 to the resulting figure. If, for example, you wish to convert 50 °C into Fahrenheit, you figure as follows:

50 divided by 5 equals 10
10 times 9 equals 90
90 plus 32 equals 122

Therefore, 50 °C equals 122 °F.

To convert Fahrenheit to centigrade, you reverse the process. You deduct 32 from the given Fahrenheit temperature, divide the resulting figure by 9 and multiply what's left by 5; that will give you the corresponding centigrade temperature. However, we have done all this for you throughout the Burda cook books. Just to show you the relationship between the two systems, here is a ,,bi-lingual" thermometer:

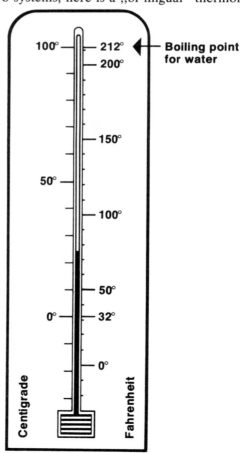

Alphabetical Index

Index by Categories